'A joyful, freeing guide to r[...]
practices to suit a range of p[...]
companion, Gemma Simmon[...] p[...]
enriching time with God. I can't wait to try it out!'
**Amy Boucher-Pye**, retreat leader and author of *7 Ways to Pray*

'In her wise advice on retreats and how to make them, Gemma Simmonds gives the Ignatian wisdom a new focus and relevance for our troubled times. In a world where isolation and loneliness so often block our capacity for healing solitude, and where the mental noise of our culture so easily makes us forget the value of the different levels and kinds of silence, this friendly advice will help and support many to begin their way back to spiritual depth and balance.'
**Laurence Freeman OSB**, The World Community for Christian Meditation, <www.wccm.org>

'This is a beautiful book, overflowing with inspirational insight and practical teaching communicated with wisdom, gentleness and simplicity. It will draw you into a practice of retreat that will lead to a deeper awareness of the presence of the divine. Gemma captures the missional essence of God by illuminating an inner life, nourished by retreat, which will affect the outward expression of faith.'
**Brian Heasley**, International Prayer Director, 24-7 Prayer

'There is a haunting sentence at the heart of Gemma Simmonds' book. She writes, "We can sometimes go for months putting one foot in front of another and not really picking up the patterns of consolation and desolation within our daily life". This apparent sleep-walking through our lives won't make us bad people, but the inference is that we become dominated by anxieties of all kinds until we have become disconnected: from God, from one another and from our very self. This would be for us all a life half lived, a lonely life. At the same time, we greet one another with the words "Are you keeping busy?" as if this has become our very survival mechanism – keeping busy.

These pages are written for everyone. For those who get it, and those who don't. For those who have time, and those who don't. It is especially helpful for people living their lives at a pace, who recognize their need to reflect and yet are really not helped by the thought of a period of seclusion in a nearby retreat house. If you don't know Gemma or haven't heard her speak at a conference, let me give you a sense of the author. Gemma doesn't make the frequent mistake of separating the heavenly and earthly realms. For her, emulating the poet Gerard Manley Hopkins, the world is charged with the grandeur of God. Her book has its head above the clouds in the sunshine and its feet on the rain-soaked cobbles. Gemma's book reminds us not to confuse the hiddenness of God for the absence of God. God is waiting for us inside our daily routines. Gemma will help us to tune in to the ever-present God who is waiting patiently in the shadow beside us.

Perhaps why I most appreciate this work is the breadth of scholarship that sits just behind the very accessible advice. Gemma's wisdom is wonderfully practical, providing insights into ways we can build retreat experiences into our lives. To do this, we are entreated to follow guidance from the Scriptures, from saints, popes, mystics, poets, songwriters and contemporary authors. We learn from the spiritual masters such as St Ignatius and, at the same time, are given all sorts of practical tips suited to our contemporary lifestyles.

Gemma may have written this book recently, but its wisdom comes from years of her own pondering. The gathered prayer, study and wisdom here are obvious. There is no doubt that following the advice in this book will bring about human flourishing: being ourselves, yet more fully alive!'

**David Wells**, author, internationally renowned speaker, lecturer and teacher, <www.davidwellslive.com>

**Gemma Simmonds** is a sister of the Congregation of Jesus. She is a senior research fellow at the Margaret Beaufort Institute of Theology in Cambridge, where she teaches Christian spirituality, and is Director of the Religious Life Institute. She is an honorary fellow of Durham University and past president of the Catholic Theological Association of Great Britain. An international speaker and lecturer, she has been a missionary in Brazil and a chaplain at the universities of Cambridge and London, as well as a chaplaincy volunteer at Holloway Prison for 25 years. She is a regular broadcaster on religious matters on the BBC, Radio Maria England and other radio and television networks. Her book, *The Way of Ignatius*, was published by SPCK for Lent 2019 and was serialized as the Lenten retreat on *Pray As You Go* (at: <https://pray-as-you-go.org>) She is also the author of *Treasuring God's Word*, which was published by Pauline Books and Media in 2020.

# DANCING AT THE STILL POINT

Retreat practices for a busy life

Gemma Simmonds

FORM

First published in Great Britain in 2021

Form
36 Causton Street
London SW1P 4ST
www.spck.org.uk

*British Library Cataloguing-in-Publication Data*
A catalogue record for this book is available from the British Library

ISBN 978–0–281–08471–5
eBook ISBN 978–0–281–08472–2

1 3 5 7 9 10 8 6 4 2

Typeset by Manila Typesetting Company
First printed in Great Britain by Jellyfish Print Solutions

eBook by Manila Typesetting Company

Produced on paper from sustainable forests

For the many open-hearted pilgrims who have given me the great privilege of accompanying them and, in doing so, have taught me so much about God's delight in being with us.

Also, especially, for the always wise, kind and immensely courageous Stan Dye, Missionary of Africa, who was the best of supervisors and who went home to God during the writing of this book.

# Contents

# Introduction

When this book was first mooted in 2019, we decided to aim it at over-busy Christians of all traditions and other interested spiritual explorers seeking help in undertaking a do-it-yourself retreat. This means creating time and space to let God be present to them in the pressured life that has become today's norm. It never occurred to any of us planning the book that it would end up being written and published in the midst of a global pandemic which would turn our busy world upside down. In some ways, many people would appear to have been living in retreat conditions since the lockdown came upon us, whether they chose this or not. The spiritual discipline of many retreats to withdraw from normal social interaction, close off the outside world and embrace solitude as a way of making space to encounter God has been visited with a vengeance on the general population. For some it has been an intolerable burden, while others have found it a God-given opportunity to stand back from normal daily pressures and to embrace a different pace of life.

The French have a saying that it is necessary to *reculer pour mieux sauter.* Roughly translated, this means making a greater leap forwards by taking a few steps back. I would not wish in any way to belittle the heartbreaking struggles of many individuals and families for whom the pandemic has meant seeing their future cast in doubt and their relationships placed under severe strain. But even amid all the loneliness, anxiety and frustration, many have found an opportunity to reassess their lives and consider what is really of value and what can be let go of without regret. What seemed a good idea for a book a year ago now looks like a vital strategy for creating the conditions in which to discern a way through an uncertain present to a future full of hope (Jeremiah 29.11).

In his encyclical *Saved by Hope*, Pope Benedict speaks of the Christian message being not only informative but also performative. The gospel is not simply information to be made known but also something that makes things happen and is life-changing. He speaks of the dark door of time being thrown open so that those who have hope can live differently.[1]

The 'dark door of time' has most brutally and unexpectedly been thrown open by the global pandemic and none of us knows what lies beyond it. A retreat gives us the opportunity to step off the conveyor belt of daily routine and stop to ask ourselves how we might live in a way that is more life-giving. My hope is that this book will help those inexperienced in making retreats to seize the opportunity and step forwards on to the path that leads to the great adventure of closer companionship with God.

# 1

# Fantastic retreats and how to find them

## Not a self-help programme

No longer the preserve of the professionally religious, retreats have become more mainstream in recent years, so that they are not only for religious believers but also for those with no definite religious affiliation, but who are serious about deepening their spiritual life. People of all kinds have become uneasily aware that the pace of modern life has become damagingly toxic and disconnected. Magazines are full of wise advice from athletes, TV personalities and lifestyle gurus about living more simply. Deaths from stress-related and addictive illnesses are rising inexorably and, despite life for many becoming considerably easier than in previous generations, society in general has seen an exponential rise in depressive conditions and mental disorders. Greater prosperity has not brought us peace. The trickle-down theory of economics has not prevented the dramatic poverty on our own doorstep, with thousands accessing food banks and emergency shelters. Endemic loneliness is spreading as people become separated from their families and communities of origin, with loneliness likely to increase the risk of death by

26 per cent and be associated with an increased risk of early mortality, as well as cognitive decline and dementia.[1] It is a sense of not knowing where to come home to and be at rest that turns many people towards the inner journey. The industry that lies around mindfulness offers a dizzying array of options for those wishing to live more intentionally, but not everyone can afford the money or the time to indulge in the intensity of a silent retreat in a specialized retreat house.

In 'mind, body and spirit' retreats, the energy for growth and change generally comes from the effort and personal resources of the person making the retreat. In a Christian retreat, the starting point is precisely that we cannot help ourselves. Pulling ourselves up by our spiritual or moral bootstraps simply doesn't work. This is the fundamental premise of the Twelve Steps programme, which has Christian origins, and the first three steps of which acknowledge:

1  We admitted we were powerless over alcohol – that our lives had become unmanageable.
2  Came to believe that a Power greater than ourselves could restore us to sanity.
3  Made a decision to turn our will and our lives over to the care of God as we understood Him.[2]

This is not to suggest that people wanting to make a retreat do so because they are struggling with alcohol or substance abuse, though that may be true in individual cases. Nor am I suggesting that serious substance addiction can be

2

dealt with simply by going on retreat from time to time. But there is considerable wisdom in the Twelve Steps programme for anyone seeking a better life balance. Addictions come in many types and intensities, including all types of 'disordered attachments' and habits that are impossible to break on our own, whether toxic patterns of relationship or damaging lifestyle habits and destructive ways of treating ourselves or others. Having a religious faith may not always help in this respect. The insistent attachment to toxic images of God can be among the most deeply entrenched and hardest to overcome 'addictions', embedded from childhood and immensely challenging to disentangle. They legitimize appalling amounts of self-hatred and harsh inner judgement, which leads to the scapegoating either of oneself or of those considered beyond redemption. Negative ways of thinking that weaken faith, hope and love within us can all be classified as addictive and destructive patterns which make our life less than manageable.

It always pains me to see spiritual books, whether classics or modern works, lurking in the self-help section of bookshops. The point that any decent book of Christian spirituality makes is precisely that we cannot redeem ourselves. That was the whole point of the incarnation, when Jesus chose to enter fully into the human condition in order to redeem it from within. Human beings are wired for friendship with God. The desire to enter into and nourish that friendship is a desire to become our deepest, truest self, which comes from God's initiative, not our endeavour. A retreat is not about self-help but about transformative encounter with the wholly Other.

# Making space

There are few better ways of democratizing spirituality than making a retreat. A retreat is a vote of confidence in our own capacity to hear and respond to the God who dwells within us. Whether it entails going to a specialist retreat house, joining a retreat online or deciding to make a DIY retreat, we take a longer or shorter time out of our normal schedule and make space for God and for our spiritual life, whether on a daily, weekly or monthly basis. A retreat in daily life means finding God not only on the mountaintops but also down in the midst of the marketplace. It will still be necessary to create space and quiet for God to be able to get a word in edgeways, but we can learn to create our own 'inner monastery' or 'inner desert' in which we can experience closer encounter with God and make more life-giving choices for ourselves. The prophet Isaiah tells us: 'The Lord waits to be gracious to you . . . blessed are all those who wait for him' (Isaiah 30.18).

Julian of Norwich describes God as 'hanging about' us. We are the ones who need to choose to make time and space for this relationship – God is 'hanging about' all the time, in the hope that we will want to engage. There is nothing stopping us but our own inner judgements that 'I'm just too busy' or 'Retreats aren't for people like me' or 'I don't deserve this – other people have greater needs right now' or any other voice that tells us we aren't worth it.

This book is presented in chapters with a thematic approach to enable readers to work through it at their own pace. A reader can decide to use the book over a sustained period of time or just use it as a guide gradually to develop better spiritual habits. It has suggestions at the end of each section to help tailor the material to the time available. The overall aim is to help the readers to realize that a rich life of prayer is possible for ordinary people, and to choose to create some time and space to let God be present to them even in a busy life. Inner stillness isn't only accessible via long hours of silent contemplation. The human soul is like a musical instrument that, if kept well tuned, can make glorious music at the mere touch of God's hand. When we take time to pay attention to what is going on within and around us, beholding God in whatever way we catch a glimpse, and allowing ourselves to be beheld in turn, we discover the potential to become fully alive that each human being carries. This is not an esoteric activity of the spiritually privileged few but something easily accessible that comes naturally when we allow space for it. I hope this helps those reading the book to take their first steps into the adventurous territory of making a retreat for themselves.

## Key questions

A good place to begin a DIY retreat is by asking yourself what it is you hope for, what you are seeking. John's Gospel begins with the religious authorities asking John the Baptist, 'Who are you?' On the following day, John identifies Jesus to his disciples as the Lamb of God. We in our turn need to ask God, 'Who are you for me? And who am I for you?' The key question behind any retreat has to be, 'Where do I find God? Where should I look? How will I know if my search has been successful?' The answer, as in Jesus' response to the disciples who ask him this, is always, 'Come and see.' The disciples begin to see by spending time with Jesus. As I reflect on this question it becomes one about where and who Jesus is in my life and what impact this might have on the way I choose to live.

Repeatedly in the Gospels people appear, wanting to see Jesus, to know who he is. They enter into conversation with him, willingly or unwillingly. Many, like the Roman centurion or Zacchaeus, come with prepared speeches. Others, like Nicodemus, come with hidden motives. Others, like the woman of Samaria, come laden with their own preconceptions. Through imaginative contemplation we move from being onlookers to becoming participants in the story, in an encounter that leads to change, according to our own personal character and circumstances.

In Luke's Gospel, Jesus meets a man possessed by demons and totally alienated from himself. For years he has lived naked among the tombs, gashing himself and raving in his distress. Jesus performs a spectacular act of healing and the man, once again restored to himself and to society, begs to become a disciple, but Jesus tells him to go home to his family and proclaim there what God has done for him (Luke 8.26–39). Later in the same Gospel, Jesus meets a young man from the ruling class, the very antithesis of the naked, helpless and self-alienated Gerasene demoniac. He is privileged, educated and wealthy, master of all he surveys, but he knows that there is something missing from his life and comes to Jesus seeking an answer. Jesus invites him to give up everything that is shackling him to his securities and to come on the road with him as a disciple. The young man cannot let go of his wealth and goes away sad (Luke 18.18–30). Both men in their own way want to follow Jesus. One needs what he has lost to be restored to him in order to live his life to the full, while the other needs to let go of his security in order to stop being a prisoner of it. One chooses freedom, while the other chooses to remain in chains. There is not a one-size-fits-all cure as far as Jesus is concerned. What is liberty for one is enslavement for another. God comes to meet us as we are and treats each one of us as an individual whose story is unique. This is why making a retreat in which there is time for me to be on my own with God, speaking as one friend to another, is so important. My story is unique to me, and God meets me where I am.

## 'Where are you?'

If part of a retreat consists in asking God, 'Where are you?', then God also appears to be asking us the same question, not because God doesn't know the answer but because we need to ask that question of ourselves and give our own answer. In the third chapter of the book of Genesis, the man and his wife hide themselves from God's presence when they realize that they are naked (Genesis 3.8–10). Good people with positive spiritual intentions can have a remarkably ambivalent attitude towards getting up close and personal with God. They say that they want to deepen their relationship with God, but often run away and hide at the first hint that God might be interested in reciprocating. There is something enchanting in the thought that the first human beings were able to hear the sound of God walking in the garden. This suggests that, in our primordial state, we human beings are born naturally sensitive to God's presence and instinctively able to tune in to wherever God can be found. But the story warns us that there is also something within us that reacts negatively to the thought of a close encounter. It is born of shame and fear: we fear to be found naked and so we hide. That spiritual nakedness is about being known as we truly are. For some, there is a profound longing to be known, recognized, acknowledged and accepted. Others are terrified of being left with nowhere to hide, either from God or from their unmasked illusions. God is not fooled by the many masks that we wear and the disguises that we adopt. God does not love us despite our sinfulness, still less on condition that we are healed from it before we dare come into his presence. God loves us precisely because of our sinfulness and understands it better than we do ourselves.

In his bestselling book *God of Surprises*, Jesuit Gerry W. Hughes claims, 'The facts are kind, and God is in the facts.'[3] By this he means that there is nothing about our lives that cannot be redeemed and accepted in God's loving wisdom and providence. The figure of the wounded healer is well known in spiritual literature, if not always well supported and appreciated in public life. I learned a great deal from accompanying a recovering alcoholic through an extended retreat, who often used the acronyms of Alcoholics Anonymous. One of these is HALT, which stands for 'Never let yourself get too Hungry, Angry, Lonely or Tired'. It is under these conditions that addictive habits become most insistent as our need for comfort kicks in. Many very good and generous people live in a semi-permanent state of hunger, anger, loneliness and tiredness. The hunger may stem from meals skipped while they are busy saving the universe, or it may be for nourishment of the soul through art, music, silence, simple time off. Standing back a little, even from the most urgent pastoral or family needs, taking time and space to attend to our own inner life, can make a huge difference to the impact we have, simply by our presence, without needing to become the world's messiah.

Psychologist Carl Jung urges us to awaken to the wisdom that lies within all of us if only we will attend to our inner process, because it is there that we will find the divine life at work within us. One version of Psalm 84 says, 'Blessed are those whose strength is in you, whose hearts are set on pilgrimage' (Psalm 84.5, NIV). Jung's own experience as a psychotherapist and his accompaniment of people who had the courage to look reflectively at their own lives convinced him that those pilgrims who have the courage to set out on the journey find that they are able to travel by an energy that comes simultaneously from within and outside themselves. He believed that what he called 'the pattern of God' existed in every human being as the source of all our energies for transformation and transfiguration. I cannot promise that transformation and transfiguration of our natural being will automatically follow from one or even several retreats. Such transformation and transfiguration is a lifetime's work, and it needs our daily attention as well as occasional times of exclusive focus, but those times of exclusive focus can allow us space to map out the next section of the road.

# Wrestling with God

The German priest and painter Sieger Köder painted naive but vivid depictions of biblical encounters between God and human beings. I have worked with these paintings for many years and one of my favourites is of Jacob wrestling with God's messenger – an angel or God himself.[4] Jacob and the mysterious adversary are at the ford of the Jabbok, locked in close combat. Jacob's left hand is pulling the angel towards him, as if in embrace, while the right hand is pushing the angel away. The angel is either lifting Jacob up out of the water or attempting to push him down under – it's hard to tell which. They look as if they might be fighting or dancing, struggling or embracing. Jacob's face and that of the shadowy figure are mirror images of one another. In Genesis, Jacob says to the one wrestling with him, 'I will not let you go, unless you bless me' (Genesis 32.26). To ask a blessing of a stranger is to ask the stranger to reveal himself in some sense. Effectively, Jacob is saying, 'I will not let you go unless you tell me who you are.' The angel does not reveal his own identity but offers Jacob a new name and identity. He is no longer Jacob but Israel. Effectively the angel/God is replying, 'I will not tell you who I am, but I will tell you who you are.'

Entering into retreat may be to show a willingness to wrestle with God or with our own struggles to get a sense of who or what God is. St Augustine of Hippo said that if we understand God, we can be sure that it is not God we are understanding. Many of us discover within ourselves the same ambivalence towards God as Jacob displays, saying to God, 'Come close, but not too close – I don't want you to take me too far out of my comfort zone.' Our struggles with the one who is so close to us yet remains ever unknown may last a lifetime. Our faith may consist in progressively losing any sense at all of who and how God is for us. At a particularly difficult moment in their following of Jesus, the disciples found themselves faced with many of their companions deciding to abandon him because of his 'intolerable language' (John 6.60, NJB). Jesus turns to Peter and asks, 'What about you? Will you go away too?' Jesus' doctrine of the bread of life was probably equally horrifying and incomprehensible to Peter. One can almost see the shrugging shoulders, 'Lord, to whom shall we go?' It's as if Peter is thinking that if there were anyone else he could go to, he would gladly give it a try, but he knows that there is no one else. This is the one, even if following him is becoming increasingly hard. In another painting of Köder's we see the same opposing hand gestures as in the painting of Jacob. This time the painting is of Peter, as Jesus kneels down to wash his feet. One hand is on Jesus' shoulder, pulling him close and embracing him, while the other hand is raised in shocked resistance. We may find ourselves in a similar position at times, both wanting closeness with God and fearing what that might ask of us. We need not be afraid. Julian of Norwich tells us that God finds in us 'his homeliest home'. If that is true, then in God we will find a similar home, where we are always welcome and never a stranger.

## Suggestions

- If reading this has made you decide to try making a retreat at home, how do you plan to go about it? You will need to make time and find a space in which you can be alone and reflective. Can you do this at home or do you need to get out of the house in order to do it? How do you need to organize your time? What resources do you have or do you feel you need?

Practical points: if trying to find some kind of retreat space at home, it's important to distance yourself from whatever will try to lure your attention back to the many things clamouring for your attention (I don't mean children, who are in a special category of their own). Switch off your computer, turn your phone to silent, setting holding messages if necessary, so that you can be sure that nothing vital is missed. If possible, spend this time away from your desk/kitchen/garage or wherever you habitually work. Decor helps, and a candle or some gentle music can be an aid to prayer, but the most important factor is the time. If you can't do this indoors, go outside and take a walk, even if you end up sitting on a park bench for most of it.

- There are many excellent resources available on the internet for helping you with reflective time. One of the best is IgnatianSpirituality.com (at: <www.ignatianspirituality.com/ignatian-spirituality-online>).

In the following chapters we will talk about preparing bodily for a retreat and making use of different tools for prayer and reflection. In this chapter we have talked about God, but have also talked of some people's preference to refer to a Higher Power. How do you respond to language about God or about a transformative and transfiguring power? Do you believe that such power is accessible? How might you go about opening yourself to it?

- At various points in the gospel Jesus asks people, 'What do you want? What are you looking for?' How would you answer such a question? If you like list-making, make a list or else draw or paint this or find any other way you like to articulate your desires at this time.
- A helpful list of questions for a review of a time of prayer and reflection can be found in the excellent *Orientations* by the late John Veltri SJ.[5] Here is one list.
    - What happened inside me during the period of prayer?
    - How did I feel about what went on?
    - What was my mood, change in mood . . . what feelings flowed through me?
    - What thoughts came in and out of my mind . . . where was I drawn to dwell?
    - How were God and I present or absent to each other?
    - Did I receive the grace I was seeking?
    - Is there some point I should return to in my next period of prayer?

# 2

# Making room

Making a retreat is not about hunkering down into some defensive bunker against the world, but about stepping back from things in order to discover strengths and resources to which we don't always allow ourselves access. Some people find it necessary to go right away and cut themselves off from all other distractions and calls on their attention. A retreat can be an important part of the preparation for making a significant choice or for working out how that choice is to be lived out in practice. Prior to becoming leaders of their respective countries, both Julius Nyerere in Tanzania and Garret Fitzgerald in Ireland are reported to have made retreats. We are constantly taking in information, consciously and unconsciously, but many of us are less skilled at processing and interpreting it. The human mind and soul are not some infinite filing cabinet into which endless data can be crammed. Some measure of sifting and sorting needs to be done in order to make sense of the huge amount of data that comes our way. In the same way, religious believers carry around a considerable amount of religious information in their heads, but the journey from head to heart can be a long and challenging one and many travellers get stuck in the waiting room without ever quite boarding the train.

The silence and withdrawal of a retreat can take many forms and while some people take a week or even a full month to go into complete silence, others make retreats in daily life, with the time for prayer and reflection carved out amid their normal schedules and commitments. This book is principally aimed at people seeking to make a retreat of whatever form in their own surroundings. No one ever learned to appreciate a great work of art by pressing their nose against it. But while stepping back can help us to focus better, withdrawal is not an end in itself. It's about creating space, both physical and mental, for effective reflection to take place. Our relationship with God works very like any other kind of relationship. If we never take time to be with those we love, to listen to them and to express our own feelings, the relationship will get stuck and never move beyond the initial stages. We don't need our surroundings to be perfect in order to make a helpful retreat. It can become a distraction from the real thing to spend all our energy getting the plainchant or the whale music and the scented candles and the decor just right, rather like preparing for an intimate dinner with someone we love and getting so caught up in the menu and the table decorations that we forget to welcome the beloved to the meal itself.

Some people's work and family commitments don't make the finding of time and space at home possible. They develop habits like sitting in the car for half an hour to be quiet with God before going home from work, or locking themselves in the bathroom and having a leisurely bath in God's presence, while the family rampages outside the door. During the Soviet era, a sister of my congregation was imprisoned for 14 years in the Gulag. Herded into a small space with over 80 other women from every point on the political and religious spectrum in highly unsanitary conditions, she found herself in tense circumstances far removed from the quiet and peace of her convent. Sister Clara suggested that they make a retreat together before they ended up killing one another. They decided on a programme of reflection and sharing during the six weeks of Lent, each from her own perspective, whenever their prison routine allowed for it. The time spent, even under these impossible conditions, proved the foundation of greatly improved relationships and resilience within the group as the women mined the depths of their own hearts and beliefs to find hidden sources of strength. Each found a way, both through her own beliefs and values and through listening to those of others, to move beyond the horror and the cruelty of the Soviet prison system. Even in circumstances such as these, the enrichment of a retreat is possible.

In 1967, at a gathering of 30,000 hippies in San Francisco, American psychologist Timothy Leary advocated that they 'turn on, tune in, drop out'. The practices that went with his famous mantra are light years away from the practice of retreat advocated here, but there are some similarities with retreats. A retreat is an opportunity to 'turn off' the endless drone of advertising and the audio and visual white noise of the computer screen with its barrage of information, fake news and trivial connections. This opens up the possibility of 'turning on and tuning in' to the divine life that simmers within our own deeper thoughts and imaginings, which often remain stunted and unfulfilled through lack of proper attention. If, as Plato quotes Socrates as saying, 'the unexamined life is not worth living', then many of us experience life at a fraction of its potential value, because so much of it goes unreflected on. When we tune in, we may find buried treasures, or warning signs that should not be ignored. We may also find that, far from dropping out, tuning in may help us to dive more deeply into the focused and purposeful life we have been wanting to live.

In 2009, entrepreneur Rob Parsons published a book called *The Heart of Success: Making it in business without losing in life*.[1] In it he described people who are cash rich but time poor, working in high-earning jobs and living in high-income households but without the time to enjoy the wealth that they have accumulated. Seeking success in the professional sphere so that they can have a secure and happy personal life, ironically they end up having no personal life to speak of. Jesus' parable in Luke 12.15–21 tells of the rich fool who spends his life accumulating wealth only to die before he can enjoy it. Having no time to live meaningfully may not only be a question of financial and work pressure but also one of what we think of as the fullness of life itself. What constitutes a meaningful life for me? What permissions do I need to give myself in order to be quiet for a time and to take stock of my life? What are my deepest longings, and can I allow myself space and time to nurture and develop them?

Some years ago, I attended a retreat given by a Jesuit priest to a religious community running a very busy boarding school. Throughout it he repeated the mantra, 'Remember, the graveyards are full of indispensable people.' Religious people have often thoroughly schooled themselves into thinking that their own needs must always be subordinated to the needs of those they serve. Women in many cultures have also been socialized into thinking this, though it is a state of mind not always arising from gender or religion. Life circumstances can turn men, women and even children into full-time carers whose own needs habitually get buried in the pressure of seeing to those of others. Busy parents can't always be switching off and taking time to put their feet up and have a cup of tea, but we can often do a better job of caring for others if there has been some necessary self-nurture as well. In the absence of extended family or a fully effective care system, people sometimes have few choices when faced with the responsibility of care within the home. In the workplace it can be similar, with major responsibilities falling, without obvious support, on the shoulders of an individual. But time and space for reflection can pay dividends well beyond the expenditure of the time taken. The graveyards are indeed full of indispensable people who have died before they ever fully lived.

The wise father of a friend of mine coined the phrase, 'If you're "too busy", you're too busy.' This may seem self-evident, but it's worth asking ourselves how often and why we say to ourselves and others that we are too busy for something that seems an indulgence in comparison to the highly important tasks with which we fill our days. Are they so important? Would making another choice really be so indulgent?

At the end of his parable, Jesus has God asking the rich fool a killer question: 'But God said to him, "You fool! This very night your life is being demanded of you. And the things you have prepared, whose will they be?"' (Luke 12.20–21).

St Ignatius of Loyola asks a similar killer question in his Spiritual Exercises: if you knew that this was the last day of your life, how would you wish to have spent your life? Few of us would find ourselves regretting that we had not spent more time at meetings or writing reports, commuting to work, putting out the bins, dusting the furniture or de-worming the dog. When the passenger planes were hijacked on 9/11, most people who had the time and opportunity to do so are reported to have rung their loved ones to tell them how much they loved them. Personal or family illness, financial constraints or circumstances beyond our control can curtail our life choices and make it impossible for us to fulfil our initial dreams. But it may be that there are more ways of living the deeper life we long for than we realize. Perhaps we have a gift or a talent that has remained undeveloped. The opportunity or the capacity may now lie behind us, but could that capacity flourish in a different way? A gift for cooking may turn into creative cake-baking or brewing, working in a soup kitchen or with a food bank. A gift for music may be expressed in joining a choir (even an online one) or in attending a singalong group in a care home or joining a music appreciation class. All of this is part of God's call to life lived abundantly. A retreat gives us the space to reconnect with what matters most to us and to examine the way in which we are living a life consistent with our deepest desires and values. It enables us to reflect on where our life may appear to have drifted from its mooring into the meaningless shallows. Artistic expression is not a luxury, but part of our deepest, most instinctive self-expression of what it means to be alive at all. With those for whom a relationship with God is key to their lives, all this allows God space to speak in the silence of our hearts and to invite us to the fullness of life that is his promise.

## Nature as nurture

At the beginning of his Spiritual Exercises, St Ignatius places his foundational belief in the purpose of the created world. He observes that human beings are made to know, love and serve God and that everything in creation is there to enable this knowledge, love and service of God to flourish. This suggests a powerful link between human beings and the natural world surrounding them.[2] One of the greatest tragedies to befall us is disconnection from the natural world. Many people living in cities at the beginning of the lockdown following the outbreak of COVID-19 began to notice how, with the removal of air and road traffic, the sounds of nature began to attract their attention. A whole world that had previously lain silent and unnoticed suddenly burst in on their consciousness. People were stunned by the beauty of birdsong, the loud, insistent humming of bees and the chirruping of squirrels. All of this was present before, only most of us were too busy to notice and the noise of our busyness drowned it out. The internet became full of films of wild animals entering spaces that had been barred to them by traffic and the excluding presence of human beings going about their business. It was as if the pandemic had suddenly revealed to us a whole parallel world that had also been going about its own business around, above and below us, but had remained invisible to our blinkered eyes.

To some Christians this may all sound very New Age and Flower Power. Surely faith is about being saved. But Carl Jung points out that a religion based on salvation will chiefly elicit the emotions of fear and trembling, while a religion based on wonder will chiefly elicit the emotion of gratitude. Salvation and wonder are not incompatible with one another. In the Hebrew Scriptures the Prophets and the Psalms are constantly reminding God's people that loss of faith comes from a loss of collective memory. They are constantly urging the people to 'remember the things that the Lord has done'. These are the manifestations of God's intervention in history, as understood by the Israelites within their own ancestral story. But they also include creation itself, from the creation of the universe out of nothing to the smallest detail of the flora and fauna that the Israelites saw all around them. The book of Proverbs depicts wisdom as a master worker, ever at play in God's presence and delighting to be with the human race (Proverbs 8.22–31). Psalm 104 recounts in detail the wonders of the natural world as the expression of God's love, including the creation of Leviathan simply as the expression of God's love of play.

One of the best ways to begin a retreat is to take time to re-centre ourselves within the created world. It isn't necessary to live in the depths of the country or even to have a large garden. It's a question of paying attention and this can be done from the window of a high-rise flat or in a local park. Whether we spend time watching a spider weaving its web or a bird preening its feathers, a squirrel burying a nut or a cat sleeping in the sun, the world of animals can reveal their concentration on the 'nowness' of things, which can bring us back to an appreciation of what an eighteenth-century spiritual writer called 'the sacrament of the present moment'.[3] Theologically speaking, a sacrament is a sign that makes real what it signifies. If only we allow ourselves to concentrate on the 'realness' of the present moment, it can overwhelm us with the richness of the gift and the generosity of the Giver.

Some years ago, I had the privilege of swimming with dolphins in Kaikoura in the South Island of New Zealand. We were encouraged to put our heads underwater and sing to attract their attention. I did as I was told and immediately was surrounded by a group of dolphins swimming rapidly round me in circles. What struck me powerfully was the intelligence in their faces and the immediate sense of kinship that I had with them. If I was gazing in wonder at them, they were also gazing at me with considerable interest. I had no sense of 'otherness' but, on the contrary, a strong sense of being considered and measured by creatures as aware and intelligent as myself. It was one of the strongest senses of connection I have ever felt, and my principal emotion was one of immense gratitude. It can be disconcerting to be stared at, whether by a dolphin, a cat or a small child. Their gaze is unfiltered by considerations of social politeness or self-consciousness. Such a gaze interrogates us and provokes us to interrogate ourselves. Who am I, really? What am I here for? What am I doing with my life?

In the first book of Kings, the prophet Elijah is fleeing for his life across the desert, making for the holy mountain of Horeb, when God asks him, 'What are you doing here,

Elijah?' (1 Kings 19.1–13). Later on, Elijah experiences three of the natural phenomena in which ancient people often detected the presence of the divine: earthquake, wind and fire. However, God is not manifest in the power of nature but in the sound of a gentle breeze or, as another translation has it, a 'still, small voice'. Nature can speak to us through awe and magnificence but just as often, in daily life, can offer us insights into the miracle of life itself when we simply notice the simultaneous otherness and kinship of our fellow creatures, great and small.

Taking a flower or a piece of fruit and simply sitting with it for ten minutes, slowly looking at it, touching, smelling and eating it (if edible) can be a revelation. If wonder and a sense of amazement can come from concentrating for ten minutes on one daffodil or apple, imagine what an hour's walk can do when really open to the full impact of creation all around us. This is 'turning on and tuning in', and the rewards are powerful. It's not just about staring at beauty, which we can do by looking at a nature calendar or watching a wildlife programme on television. It's about entering deeply into the mystery of our creatureliness and allowing the mutuality of that creatureliness to inhabit and challenge our consciousness via each one of our senses.

A sense of our own createdness by God can also be powerfully brought home to us by connecting with the natural environment. It isn't necessary to roam the country looking for the perfect spot. A bus trip or a visit to a nearby park or churchyard, a local canal or an allotment can work just as well. Nature doesn't so much speak as shout at us when we allow it time and space to do so. In the later years of his

life, when busy as the leader of the worldwide religious order that he founded, St Ignatius of Loyola lived in Rome
and was no longer able to wander through the countryside
at will. He took, instead, to standing on his balcony at night
and looking up at the stars, finding space to be still and feel
the touch of God. Looking up at the stars, or just the moon,
can give us a sense of proportion. As Psalm 8 puts it:

> When I look at your heavens, the work of your
>       fingers,
>    the moon and the stars that you have
>       established;
> what are human beings that you are mindful of
>       them,
>    mortals that you care for them?
> Yet you have made them a little lower than God,
>    and crowned them with glory and honour.
> (Psalm 8.3–5)

Stunning wildlife programmes are widely available on our
computer and television screens, but how many of us think
of using them as material for prayer? As an introduction to
retreat, taking time to see such a programme in slow motion, to stop the screen and simply contemplate the wonders
presented, is as good a form of prayer and praise as any. This
is the panoramic view that allows us to see how, as the Jesuit
poet Gerard Manley Hopkins put it, 'The world is charged
with the grandeur of God.'[4]

Making space to expose ourselves to that grandeur, to
allow it to call out from us a response of wonder and delight,

is a prayer in itself. In the book of Daniel, three young Jews saved from deadly peril break out into a canticle of praise of God manifest in the natural world (Daniel 3.51–90). To pray that prayer with a photographic memory of the breezes and winds or oceans and seas as we have directly encountered them can be a powerful experience, but we need to take time for our mind's eye to conjure them for us, and for the wonder to overtake us. I once invited the retreatants at the beginning of a residential retreat to go off for a long walk and then come back and write their own canticle from what they had seen and experienced on their walk or from their memory of favourite encounters with the natural world. One African retreatant wrote a love poem to the animals, trees and landscape of his own land, from which he was in political exile. It was one of the most thrilling pieces of 'personal scripture' I had ever seen, bringing the warmth and vivid beauty of Africa immediately to mind. I had no need to tell this person how to pray with nature. He had clearly been doing so instinctively since childhood.

## Prayer in retreat

Once you have found sufficient space and silence to make a retreat, whether for a day or a week or in daily life, what next? What do you actually do with the space and the silence? It's not a question of doing anything, but of letting the space and silence work on you and transform you. We can't see or hear or feel it happen, so it can be a challenge to believe that anything is, in fact, happening at all. For many people, the compulsion to fill the time and space with activity is overwhelming. The idea that doing nothing could be productive and useful is very countercultural in the industrial world. Wasting time with God feels too much like wasting time. 'Navel gazing' is a derogatory term used for this apparently pointless enterprise. In a time-poor culture it's a shocking waste of a scarce resource.

This book is principally written for those who have an active faith life or for whom the question of personal faith is of high importance. There are as many ways to pray as there are people. St Ignatius encourages us to enter into conversation with God 'as one friend to another'. He recommends 'imaginative contemplation', by which he means entering into a scriptural scene with all our senses and imagination and responding to it with our emotions as well as our thoughts.[5] Other spiritual traditions shy away from the use of mental images or of mental faculties at all and encourage the avoidance of thoughts and words in favour of a mental stillness and emptiness that many find difficult to achieve. Others recommend ruminating over the words of Scripture in what is known as *lectio divina*, or holy reading, or the use of a mantra such as the Jesus Prayer. Still others recommend the use of vocal prayer and singing. I often find myself singing hymns very loudly while driving the car when no one else is there to hear me, though I tend to avoid doing this on public transport, as it can prove disconcerting to my fellow passengers. All of this is prayer, but so are writing, painting, using clay creatively, looking prayerfully through a photograph album, and many other reflective exercises that lead our heart into conversation with God.

No one form of prayer is intrinsically 'better' than another. Prayer is not something we do for God, but something that God does for us. It's always a good thing to explore different forms of prayer, since, as with any form of self-expression, it can become stale if it doesn't move and vary as we grow and change. Prayer is not a performance. We are not the leaders but the led, not the singers but those who allow the song to be sung in us. Made as we are in God's image, we have the natural capacity to respond to God present in all aspects of creation. Our main task is to open our minds, hearts and every other physical, spiritual and intuitive sense so that we can respond to all that God has created for his praise and glory. Prayer is not an art project, though allowing ourselves to respond creatively to what God brings to our minds and hearts can be a very freeing way to enter into deeper relationship with God, the supreme artist. Prayer leads us beyond the limitations of ourselves into the wide expanse of God. We may find that our senses fail us, that we cannot summon up a single coherent thought and that our feelings remain muted. We may just have to sit the period through, aware of nothing but our own poverty. We may find that all our efforts to become silent and still are swept away in the maelstrom of thoughts and preoccupations that babble through our minds. Julian of Norwich says that God is grateful when we remember him. That means God is happy we showed up at all. We may not receive much gratification from the encounter, but our presence is what counts, and simply by giving what time and attention we can, God's grace gets to work in us beyond all our calculations and measurements.

## Suggestions

- Can you create a private space that is your own, even just for a short time? If there isn't one where you live, where would you go to have a bit of 'breathing space' where you can be confident of not being disturbed? What do you need to take with you or leave behind in order to make the best of that space?

- What strategies do you need to employ in order to safeguard some silence for yourself so as to make a retreat?

- You may like to begin with a favourite poem or song or Scripture passage to enable you to focus on God or on the 'still centre' within you. There are many websites where you can find material from the Scriptures or other sources to help you settle into prayerful reflection. Decide on how long you are going to take for this time of prayer and stick with it, even if it proves boring and difficult. After the dedicated period, perhaps over a drink or during a short walk, look back over the time and note in some way what was important, what was challenging, what you discovered or learned in that time. Keep this where you can visit it again after a subsequent time of prayer and reflection.

- Make a 'nature date' with yourself and with God. This may simply be giving yourself time to watch an animal or kick through fallen leaves, hold your hand in running water or hold a flower or a feather or a stone. What do you see, hear, feel, smell or touch? Where do these sensations take you, and what do they say to you of the creator God? Looking at one or other of the passages of Scripture given in this chapter, can you write or paint your own canticle of praise for creation?

- Where do the internal pressures come from that impel you to be or appear to be busy? Can you accept your own responsibility for being over-busy and let go of the compulsive busyness? Can you take responsibility for planning genuinely re-creative times?

# 3

# An 'inside the body' experience

Many people have written about having 'out of body experiences', when they experience themselves as dead and find themselves in some way a spectator outside their body, either watching themselves or meeting God or those whom they have loved and lost. Explanations for these phenomena range from the psycho-physical to the spiritual or paranormal. More extraordinary is the extent to which many of us are capable of living as if this life were one long 'out of the body' experience, our body treated as simply the packaging in which our self is presented to the world. We don't notice it until something malfunctions, and then we view it with disappointment and irritation, hoping that it will get itself back into gear again as soon as possible.

We live in our body, but it's possible for many of us to disconnect from our bodies and treat them as machines, expecting them to function accordingly. An occasional bit of oiling or tightening of loose bolts and we expect the whole thing to keep going automatically. In the developed world, where highly sophisticated levels of medical care are taken as the norm, we expect to find rapid help when ill, relying on experts to take care of our body's smooth functioning as if maintaining our car or domestic appliances. One of the great shocks of the pandemic has come from the global sense of helplessness in the face of a virus that few had predicted or expected. Not even our medical expertise and technology could find a rapid and reliable solution, and we suddenly became aware of our radical vulnerability. Our illusions of control and invincibility came crashing down, with normal physical interactions like a handshake or a hug suddenly becoming a potential source of contamination. It may prove a long time before we feel safe to touch one another again. But this global trauma may also alert us to the importance of living life as an 'in the body' experience, with our inner consciousness and our body in tune with one another, and our physical body the means by which we can come closer to our Creator. In the developing world, where it is routine for people to have limited access to clean water, reliable power sources and regular food, these become not casually accepted and expected commodities but the maintainers of life itself. We tend not to appreciate the full value of effective medical help and other precious resources until deprived of them.

How we are in our bodies can depend on our sensitivity to advertising pressure that constantly bombards us with images of the perfect body. This can make us hostile to our own less-than-perfect bodies, prey to eating disorders through the body-shaming that is rampant on social media. People spend thousands of pounds on needless cosmetic surgery in order to conform to what is impressed on them as the ideal for a desirable and attractive body. Eddie Cantor famously sang, 'Keep young and beautiful if you want to be loved'.[1] The implication is that those who are neither young nor beautiful are unlovable. Even if we consciously reject the propaganda of the beauty and diet industries, we carry these messages unconsciously. Neither anxiously trying to keep our bodily image under control nor giving up altogether and ignoring our bodies' legitimate needs helps us to maintain happy and healthy living. Both fail to see the body as the place in which divine–human encounter takes place. Our bodies matter when it comes to prayer. If we are trying to focus mind and heart on God while our body is uncomfortable, hungry, thirsty or in other ways in need of attention, we will find it almost impossible to find our centre.

At the beginning of any time of prayer it's important to get our bodies into a state of relaxed readiness. The Preparatory Exercises outlined below are designed to help you to relax physically and mentally before starting a prayer session. They can be used at the beginning of a dedicated 'retreat day' or at the beginning of specific times of prayer or reflection. How we are in our bodies matters when it comes to prayer and reflective times and activities. Too relaxed, and we are more likely to fall into sleep than into prayer. Too tense, and we will remain chiefly conscious of ourselves rather than God and are unlikely to be able to make sufficient space for God to approach us in the 'still, small voice' that is God's signature manner. Consciously using breathing exercises at the beginning of a time of prayer can help us to let go of habitual but unnoticed tensions. The following are ways that can help to bring us to an active sense of the presence of God:

## Preparatory Exercise one

Sit where you can have both feet on the ground, your spine straight but not rigid, your hands resting in your lap. Take a few deep breaths and allow yourself to exhale to the fullest extent. Become conscious of your breathing, allowing breaths to fill your lungs as far down as possible rather than just breathing from the top of your chest. Become aware of the sound of your breathing going in and out, the sounds outside the room where you are, not trying to focus on or exclude them, but just allowing them to be. Become conscious also of the sounds inside the room that are external to yourself: notice them, but then set them aside. Move from external sounds to those internal to yourself: perhaps your stomach is rumbling or you are conscious principally of the sound of your own breathing. Notice them but don't focus on them, simply allowing the rhythm of your breathing to slow, becoming conscious of stillness within and outside your own body.

## Preparatory Exercise two

Sit where you can have both feet on the ground, your spine straight but not rigid, your hands resting in your lap. Take a few deep breaths and allow yourself to exhale to the fullest extent. Become conscious of the sensations on the sensitive surface of your skull, moving down throughout your whole body and allowing yourself to become conscious of each part of it. Allow yourself to relax as you move that surface consciousness down through your whole body, relaxing your muscles and letting go of any tension that you carry. Travel down like this the whole length of your shoulders, arms and spine, feeling the furniture under you, the weight of your arms and hands in your lap and finally your legs, down to your feet on the ground, allowing all the weight of your body and the tension it carries to flow out through your feet. Remain still and breathing regularly, relaxing any part of your body that feels strained.

## Preparatory Exercise three

Sit where you can have both feet on the ground, your spine straight but not rigid, your hands resting in your lap. Take a few deep breaths and allow yourself to exhale to the fullest extent. Allow your breathing to become regular, the breaths exhaling being longer than the breaths inhaling. Allow your breathing to become the primary sound and feeling of which you are conscious. If, instead of sitting still, you are walking, become conscious of the rhythm of breathing as you walk and the sounds around you. Focus on the sounds and allow your pace to become relaxed but regular.

You may wonder why such exercises are included in a book on Christian retreat practices. In a number of faith traditions it is customary to make a gesture of reverence when entering a sacred place. God does not require us to acknowledge his presence by bowing and scraping, but it helps us to become conscious of being in that place where God is waiting to be gracious to us. These gestures help us to move from our normal world into one where prayer is the prime purpose, just as we would prepare for any significant meeting by preparing the room and ourselves. These and other exercises allow our full concentration to be focused on God-with-us in times of prayer and reflection.

# 'You fill up my senses'

Using our bodies to help us to pray is not just a matter of learning how to relax. Our bodies are themselves the vehicle for prayer. In 2000, the National Gallery in London put on a millennium exhibition of paintings and artefacts about the Christian story entitled 'Seeing Salvation'. No other exhibition or religious service at that time did more to explain and enhance the spiritual significance of the millennium than this one. People queued along the entire length of the gallery and down the adjacent streets to view the exhibition. Inside, you could see that many of the visitors were drawn into the paintings and artefacts not simply as objects of beauty but as articles provocative and interrogative of faith. Viewers' eyes filled with tears or their faces frowned in confusion. They bowed and crossed themselves while others simply looked on, expressionless. In a four-part television series, the gallery director, Neil MacGregor, analysed the way in which art can take us below and beyond words and images into the mystery of salvation itself. But we don't need to be an art historian to come close to God through a painting. It isn't always possible to find quiet and space in an art gallery packed with tourists, but a day or several hours in a gallery, looking at specific pictures, can be as good a way as any to make a time of retreat. A slow and meditative walk through the gallery with time to sit in front of a painting or artefact, learning about it but also relishing it in slow contemplation, can be a wonderful way to connect with the mystery of God. Such a day or session would need careful planning and also, perhaps, time outside the gallery itself for silent reflection and absorption of what has been seen, perhaps based on notes taken during the visit, as we allow our eyes to lead us into prayer and contemplation in this way.

Art may also be profoundly disturbing, provocative and startling. In 1999, Brazilian sculptor Ana Maria Pacheco was Associate Artist at London's National Gallery. She created a 19-figure installation of slightly larger-than-life polychrome figures entitled *Dark Night of the Soul*. With references to the martyrdom of St Sebastian, it centred on a naked male figure, kneeling and hooded, pierced by arrows and sur-rounded by ominous-looking henchmen, strongly reminis-cent of the enforcers of various Latin American dictatorships. Other figures made the circle wider: a naked baby, a look of innocent curiosity on his face, his mother reaching con-cerned arms out towards her child, others looking on in dif-ferent degrees of dismay or compassion at the central event or fighting among themselves. The installation's purpose was to get onlookers to walk among the figures and inter-act with them. It was an unsettling experience. I went to see the exhibition in order to interrogate it but found that it was I who was being interrogated. I was reminded of the many tortures, humiliations and degradations suffered in the world, of which we have a partial insight through the news. We may feel a passing disgust or compassion or anger, but then we move on with our lives. The art reminded me that, in a world where everything is connected, everyone is con-nected too. As John Donne reminds us, we are not an island, complete unto ourselves.[2] The pain of one is the pain of all. Prayer calls us into conversion towards a deeper humanity.

We don't have to go into art galleries to pray with art. It's still possible to spend dedicated time looking at a reproduction, allowing it to interrogate us. A retreat through art can take us out of our thoughts into the realm of instinctive response. The paintings don't have to be obviously religious. A visit to the Prado Gallery in Madrid years ago brought me face to face with Picasso's brutal depiction of the *Massacre at Guernica*. In the same museum I saw some of Goya's etchings of *The Disasters of War*.[3] Both are horrifying and bring into vivid reality the appalling human price of warfare and violence. They are hardly the stuff of a gentle and consoling time of quiet retreat, but they are a powerful means of entering into the mystery of the cross and Passion of Christ. Readers of this book will have their own ideas of visual art that might be good material for a time of retreat, whether short or extended. It would be a good way to make a time of retreat in a small group of people, choosing to look at some works of art, reflect and pray over them and then come back together, in person or online, to share what you have seen and prayed as a result. This is not about trying to outshine one another with virtuoso comments on art history, but an opportunity to share what God has revealed through the sense of sight.

People of a more technical or scientific turn of mind reading this book may feel that this retreat business is just for arty types and not for them. I was once invited to go and see a newspaper being printed late one evening. The moment came when the presses were set in motion. I am not scientifically or technically minded in the least, or generally enthused by machinery, but I found myself repressing a strong desire to clap or to burst out singing. The technological brilliance of that newspaper production line was a source of amazement and wonder, and it gave me an unexpected sense of delight in and praise for human ingenuity and the God who equally delights in it.

I had a similar response to a visit to Fermilab, the USA's particle physics and accelerator laboratory near Chicago.[4] Fermilab's strapline is, 'We bring the world together to solve the mysteries of matter, energy, space and time.' That is a fairly breathtaking endeavour and worth spending contemplative time considering. My visit round the Deep Underground Neutrino Experiment, the aim of which is to 'paint a clearer picture of the universe and how it works', took me straight back into Psalm 8 territory. This was an attempt to understand 'the heavens, the work of your fingers' and was another major encounter with the wonder of God. If you are someone whose passion is trains or planes or any other mechanical wonder, then let your interest and your eyes take you to where you can be surprised by joy and by praise of the one whose master worker is wisdom itself.

## The sound of music

St Augustine of Hippo is frequently credited with saying that whoever sings well prays twice. While we can't be certain that he did say precisely that, we do know he told his congregation there is nothing better, more useful or more holy for the faithful than singing. The famous theological axiom *lex orandi lex credendi* means that liturgy and theology are not separate, since the law of what is prayed is the law of what is believed. Prayer expressed in liturgy is expressive of belief. Music can not only enhance prayer but can actually also be prayer. A huge part of the canon of European classical music is taken directly from parts of the liturgy or contains the words of Scripture set to music. It would certainly be possible to spend a day or longer in a musical retreat, although as with art as prayer, there would be a distinction to be made between musical appreciation in the intellectual and technical sense and prayer experienced through the medium of music.

Martin Luther is credited with saying that, next to the word of God, music is the greatest treasure in the world. Praying through the sonorous delicacy of plainchant or the exhilarating uplift of a thunderous hymn can take us beyond, or perhaps more deeply into, the meaning of the words, breaking open the emotional dimension of words or giving emotional expression to words that, left on their own, often reach the mind but not the heart. Singing can be a form of *lectio divina*, in which we delve ever deeper into the meaning of Scripture by allowing the words to resonate within us, amplified and carried by the music. Particular musical settings can give voice to the soul's move from sense response to the integration of the words into our desire and will. The combination of meaning and emotion can move our will in the direction to which the words point.

In recent years, the chants from the ecumenical religious community of Taizé have become popular as a way of praying. Music can simply be used as a kind of liturgical wallpaper, a decoration that we hardly notice, but this is certainly not the purpose for which Taizé chants were written. The repetition of a short line of Scripture can help the words to embed themselves deeply in our consciousness, like the practice of the repetition of a mantra or of the Jesus Prayer of the Eastern tradition. Like visual art, music can both soothe and provoke. As with visual art, a time of retreat centred on music would need to be carefully thought out and planned. This is not about providing ourselves with endless hours of feel-good experiences. In some way we are submitting to the music, just as we submit to the art, allowing it to lead us rather than trying to control or manage our response. Music can take us far beyond the bland assent to theological propositions into the more dangerous and adventurous territory of embracing their meaning and purpose with our heart and senses. Johann Sebastian Bach knew about the limits of human musicality and the extent to which music is a gift from God, saying, 'I play the notes as they are written, but it is God who makes the music.' When we experience music as a God-given gift, through which God speaks to us beyond words, then we are experiencing prayer as powerfully as in any other way.

We have reflected on how visual art and music can lead us to God and can be powerful vehicles for contemplation. In the same way, our eyes and ears, when confronted with the beauty of nature, can also draw us into prayer. Time spent in a park or garden sitting under different trees reveals to us that different varieties make different music with their leaves. Dedicated time spent gazing at, touching and listening to trees can take us into a place of quiet and receptivity where the God who walked in the garden in the cool of the evening and the Carpenter whose hands were so in tune with wood and who hung on a tree can be present to us in new ways. Going for a meditative walk and hearing the sounds around us, feeling the ground beneath our feet, touching plants and flowers, gazing contemplatively at plants or animals, smelling the scents and tasting fruits or plants that are edible or just meditatively munching a sandwich while absorbing the beauty around us while looking out to sea or at a landscape – all these can be part of a retreat time.

## Poetry in motion

Poetry is a means of attracting our attention. It takes words and puts them together in a pattern, the sound or unexpected meaning of which takes us out of the banalities of everyday conversation into a landscape of meaning that resonates beyond the words themselves. There are powerful poets of the English language whose work, whether overtly religious or not, engages the contemplative dimension. Spending time with the seventeenth-century metaphysical poets or contemporary poets like R. S. Thomas, Mary Oliver, Micheal O'Siadhail, Seamus Heaney or Denise Levertov may help us to find a new language in which to pray. A poetry retreat can unlock the door to the hidden poetry within ourselves or to the richness of the poetic tradition of the psalms and other words of sacred Scripture. How long is it since you last slowly and meditatively read or recited a poem out loud? Working as a guest director in the Jesuit retreat house of St Beuno's in North Wales helped me to link the wondrous landscape of the Vale of Clwyd with the poetry it inspired in Gerard Manley Hopkins when he lived and studied there. We may find inspiration in any poet or

prose writer whose words help to articulate our own longings, fears, hopes and sorrows.

Engaging with poetry is necessarily a slow and contemplative business. We can't gobble down poems the way we
do business reports or information scanned from the internet. Approaching poetry or other literary works with the
same method as *lectio*, imaginative contemplation or journalling, what is important is to allow feelings and imagination to be touched, challenged and invited by the words so
that they always lead to my own dialogue with God.[5]

## Senses fail – or do they?

Senses Fail is the name of an American rock band. The words
also occur in a eucharistic hymn based on a poem written by
the medieval theologian Thomas Aquinas.[6] Aquinas states
that, when faced with Christ present in the Eucharist, sight,
touch and taste cannot be trusted. The only trustworthy
sense in this context is that of hearing, since it is through
hearing the doctrine of the Eucharist proclaimed through
the words of Scripture and theology that he can come to believe the mystery before him. While a great admirer of his
poem, I cannot agree with Aquinas that the senses are not to
be trusted when confronted with divine mystery. In the particular context of his poem, his words make sense, but touch
and taste and smell can also lead us to the God who gave
us bodies and senses so that, in some distant way, we could
intuit his presence. Psalm 141 asks God for our prayer to rise
like incense. St Paul speaks of the fragrance that comes from
knowing Christ (2 Corinthians 2.14), while for anyone who

has a finely balanced and sensitive sense of smell, a reading through the Song of Songs will conjure up a richness of presence and a delight in encounter. Elsewhere we are told to:

Send out fragrance like incense,
and put forth blossoms like a lily.
Scatter the fragrance, and sing a hymn of praise;
bless the Lord for all his works.
(Ecclesiasticus 39.14)

Any of our senses can draw us into God's presence. We are told to 'taste and see that the LORD is good' (Psalm 34.8). The slow and meditative use of our senses of taste and smell and touch can allow us to reconnect with our bodies and with our joyful sense of being lovingly and purposefully created. This is not about the worship of the body beautiful, but about learning to receive and accept our bodies as God's gift.

## Suggestions

- The following exercises are similar to the Preparatory Exercises in this chapter, but they are aimed at more than relaxation. You may like to do one of the Preparatory Exercises explained earlier if you are feeling tense or in need of a bridge between what you have been doing with your time and attention up until now, and the focus you want to find in this time of prayer and reflectiveness. Once you are focused on the here and now, take time to connect with your body, sitting with your back straight and feet on the ground, breathing yourself into a state of relaxation. Take one hand into the other and spend some time looking in wonder at it. Your hands may bear the marks of your age and how you habitually use them, with rough places and calluses, perhaps broken nails or scars of old wounds. These hands are evidence of God's gift in your own history of work and industry, efficiency and capability. Is there something that you feel drawn to say to your hands or to the God who made them? If you are bendy enough, you may also like to try this with your feet.

- You may be drawn to spend time looking at natural beauty or looking out at the place where you live: the buildings, the people, the movement of transport and machinery. All of this can speak to us of the God who gives life to the natural world and who gives us human ingenuity to be creators in our turn. You may like to plan a day or a period of time that allows you to gaze contemplatively and then spend some time in reflection, perhaps journalling or drawing or writing poetry about what you have seen and how that drew you to the Creator.

- For a retreat in an art gallery you will need to plan what you want to see and how you want to reflect on it afterwards. You may want to go from the gallery into a church or other quiet place where you can absorb what you have seen. If it is impossible to visit a gallery or an art installation, can you find a book or an online website where you can stay with some of the art that you see there? This can also be done with photographs or sculpture.

- A retreat with music will also need planning in terms of how you reflect on what you have been listening to.

A retreat with a sense of hearing can also be about listening to the sea or the sound of trees or sheep in a field. In a retreat with the senses, allow your senses to take you closer to the God who created our bodies for enjoyment. It may be that you are led to a deepened sense of praise and gratitude, or you may find that becoming more closely acquainted with your body brings you to the sorrow of having lost certain senses or faculties, or the evidence that your body is ageing or sick. What do you want to say to God about this, and what does God say in return? Take time to reflect on this and journal or express what has happened in some way.

- Our embodied selves can reveal God to us. If my body could talk to me now, what would it want to say to me about how I am and about my desire to be who I was created to be in all aspects of my life: personal and professional, about the situation I currently find myself in, the choices I have made? Do my bodily sensations bring me to an awareness of something I haven't noticed before, or something I hope for or have been trying to avoid? How does this reconnection with my body lead me into conversation with my body's creator? Notice what happens in that conversation. Look up the poem by Symeon the New Theologian, 'We Awaken in Christ's Body' (at: <www.poetry-chaikhana.com/Poets/S/SymeontheNew/ Weawakenin/index.html>). What does it say to you?

- Finally, you may find some form of physical exercise a way of entering into prayer, whether walking, swimming or exercise in a gym. To do this contemplatively, you will need to focus on being present to your body and your thoughts rather than on your fitness regime or your own personal athletic goals, making space to be aware of the God-givenness of your body and its movement. Either as you are moving or afterwards, is there some awareness to which your body leads you? You may wish to journal or communicate your feelings and thoughts to God afterwards.

# 4

# The examined life

One of the most important contributions made by St Ignatius of Loyola to Christian spirituality is the Examen, also known as the Examination of Consciousness or the Prayer of Awareness. In the rule of life of the Jesuit order, which he founded, he talks about how fledgling members are to maintain their spiritual life. He is quite prescriptive about the amount and type of prayer that they are to build into their daily routine, ensuring that, above all, those joining the Society of Jesus become men of prayer. Moving out of the novitiate into studies, there are fewer instructions about prayer, but students are reminded that study itself is to be considered an integral part of their prayer and life. When the Jesuit who has done his training is ready to move into the field of ministry the assumption is that, by that point, the habit of prayer has become ingrained. Ignatius knew that he was sending his men into colleges and universities around Europe, but also to pastoral ministries among the sick and the poor and a few to the modern-day equivalent of Mars. They were to go by sea to the furthest known reaches of the world and beyond, where often they would be some of the first Christians and Europeans to set foot among the people to whom they were sent. Here, at the missionary frontiers of the world, it might not be possible to access spiritual texts or the Scriptures, or to attend or even celebrate the sacraments. Prayer would be stripped down to its bare bones. If needs must, said Ignatius, and pastoral necessity demanded it, all these could go for a time, but what must be held on to under all circumstances was the Examen. Why did Ignatius set such store by this and what was its primary purpose?

A superficial and decontextualized reading of Ignatius's words about the Examen in his Spiritual Exercises might lead one to believe that it is a nit-picking exercise which mainly attempts to root out habits of sin by viewing one's day according to a set of moral formulae. Nothing could be further from his intention. The principal aim of the Examen is to maintain a sense of awareness of how God is present to me in my life and how I am present to or absent from God. Its fundamental aim is consolation, which does not mean being filled with happy thoughts and feelings but being led by God's grace through the circumstances of one's life to an ever-deepening sense of faith, hope and love. This comes about through experiencing even the smallest aspects of our daily life as a gift and a potential encounter with God. Some days feel nothing like God's gift. We may find ourselves struggling with huge external or inner challenges or with troubles that cannot easily be surmounted. The Examen is a way of helping us to experience God's abiding indwelling even when all around us appears to be in ruins. If Socrates was right that the unexamined life is not worth living, then the Examened life can help even the toughest life to feel worth continuing with. This is why Ignatius told his followers never to let go of this practice.

Just as there are many ways to enter into contemplative prayer, so there are many ways to make the Examen, with a whole Examen industry out there to help anyone wishing to learn how to do it. One of the most recent and comprehensive resources is Mark Thibodeaux's *Reimagining the Ignatian Examen*, which has been very usefully produced as an app as well as a book.[1] Above all, the Examen is a way to increase awareness of God's providential presence in our lives. It's a dangerous thing to apply too mechanical an understanding of God's will to the circumstances of our lives. It risks turning God into a monster when we find ourselves arguing that our deep losses, the global pandemic or the most recent natural disaster were willed on those who suffered them by God seeking to teach them some kind of lesson. It is equally desolating to argue in favour of a God who is a kind of divine mechanic, setting the machinery of the world into motion and then abandoning it to its own devices. The Examen helps us to experience the closeness of God even in a day that has been a struggle all the way. It reminds us that God is not some kind of holy varnish with which we attempt to overlay the gritty details of our everyday lives. God is in the grit and the grime, 'bruised, hurting and dirty' with us, as Pope Francis described the community of the Church.[2] It shines a light on the noticed and unnoticed gifts of each day, stirring us to praise, gratitude or a deep hope to be more united to God in our daily living. It helps us to be more in tune with our inner and our outer worlds, at the same time shining a compassionate light on the shadows of each day, both those we have cast ourselves and those cast on us by other people's choices or simply by the current circumstances of our lives. Praying with the Examen allows us to enter into honest conversation with God, with ourselves and with those we have hurt, asking for pardon, healing and the strength and insight to make better choices for the future. It also enables us to name the graces we believe we need to live a life more consistent with our best desires. It gives us the clarity to understand our own impulses and motivations and the triggers that lead us in harmful directions. If we are hungry for some necessary spiritual or bodily nourishment, angry with some unresolved conflict, lonely for wise companionship or too tired to function coherently, it enables us to see this and to take whatever action is necessary towards healing. It isn't a magic formula, but it is a helpful and consoling move towards living in greater truth.

We can sometimes go for months putting one foot in front of another and not really picking up the patterns of consolation or desolation within our daily life, feeling a low-lying sadness, anger or dissatisfaction without knowing where it's come from. Equally, we can receive blessings in the context of personal and work relationships, or simply the world around us, and not fully relish and enjoy them as we might. Like seeing life without one's spectacles on, everything is a bit of a blur and we miss the details. The Examen helps to adjust our focus so we see the details that we have previously missed. It can take about 15 minutes a day and can be done in as many ways as there are people, but it can also be the basis of a weekly or monthly retreat routine or an extended time of retreat in which we take one step a day. Thibodeaux suggests that the steps are to:

- relish
- request

- review
- repent
- resolve.

The first step is to savour with gratitude the blessings of the day, everything that I have experienced and recognize as a gift and a grace. The second is for me to pray that God's light be shone on to the day so that I can see it not as a performance-related activity of my own but as a Spirit-filled encounter. The review step consists of my allowing God to show me the day from God's perspective. I don't fall into despair or depression at my failures but see them as an opportunity to come closer to God as I recognize my poverty and need. From my repentance comes the resolve, in realistic terms, to live wiser and more life-giving choices for the future.

If you are making a retreat on your own for the first time, you may want to do an extended Examen that is a spiritual autobiography, dividing your life into sections: childhood, teenage years, leaving home and so on. You may want to do this as a diagram or to make use of a photograph album or scrapbook to help you. This can be a very telling way to answer the question, 'How did I get here? How has my life ended up where it is?' What emerges is your life story, so far as it is also the story of God's invitations throughout your life and how you have chosen to respond to them. If there are very sad or troubling moments in your past, it may be important to have someone you know and trust with whom you can go over these.

The Israelites went through something like this exercise every year at Passover, retelling their history, both the successes and the failures. This was a way to respond to the numerous times in the Scriptures that they were urged to 'remember the things that the LORD has done'. It was a way to renew their commitment to what was most important in their lives as individuals and as a nation. The psalms are remarkably frank about uncomfortable personal feelings of rage, disappointment, vengeance and despair, but also about the failures in fidelity of God's people. If an attempt to do an extended Examen causes you to face your own shadow history, it may be good to spend some time with a passage like Psalm 107. It looks at the failures in Israel's history, but at the end of each example of falling, they are reminded how God is there to meet them precisely in the shadow and the mess and to bring them out into the light again.

You may wish at the end of such a day or such an exercise to write your own creed. Looking back at your own life, what have been the principal values and beliefs that have underpinned who you are and what you have done with your life? What, or perhaps who, do you believe in? You may like to make a contract with yourself if you find that you have fallen into a pattern of living that you recognize as less than life-giving. What do you want to agree between God and yourself that you will try to do? This needs to be honest and realistic. All of us could write a contract to live the perfect life and we would break it at the first opportunity. Alcoholics Anonymous's famous mantra of 'one step at a time' makes very good psychological and spiritual sense, or, as Jesus told his disciples, 'deal with each challenge that comes your way, one day at a time. Tomorrow will take care of itself.'[3] It may be helpful to look at the following questions.

- Is there something I wish to change about my life?
- Is this something that is in my power to change?
- What would I need to do in order to make this change?

It may not be something negative that you want to change; it may be something you have always longed for, but 'the time has never been right' or you have not given yourself permission to pursue these ends. What would it take to choose this change now?

## The Examen: getting into the habit

In the Jesuit Constitutions, St Ignatius urges his men fully engaged in mission never to lose touch with the Examen. This may give the impression that lengthy contemplative prayer at a high level of absorption is solely the preserve of mystics and those who embrace the monastic or solitary life, far withdrawn from the busyness of the everyday working life that is normal for most people. It is certainly true that the monastic life sets aside more time for formal prayer than is available to most working people, or those with heavy family commitments or up to their eyes in caring or in ministry, with barely a quiet moment to call their own. But the Examen can become a contemplative habit that leads us into praying constantly, even though we are barely aware of it.

It can be difficult for us to live consciously, aware of the giftedness of life that is part of every moment. Our work may demand such a level of focus that breaking off repeatedly to talk to God is not an available option. Many jobs and tasks require concentrated thought whose interruption, even in God's direction, is distinctly unhelpful. Developing a habit of reflective prayer that makes one alert to the gift of the moment – the privilege of being able to study when so many gifted young people across the world have no such opportunity, the joy of being skilled in a particular task – all this leads to gratitude, even while continuing with the task itself. Every exercise of skill can become a source of thanksgiving, a prayer for help and support, a moment of wonder and praise. The joy and challenge of the present moment in and of itself is the stuff of prayer, whether we are weeding the garden, baking bread, typing up a report, fixing a car or wrapping up a parcel. It is true of delivering a baby, painting a house or driving a delivery van. The Examen as a spiritual habit shines a light of consciousness on the fabric of human living in all its detail by making us more aware of God's presence in those lives. Things unnoticed rise to the surface, and not only the physical and mental actuality of the moment but also the inner process that accompanies it. This in turn fixes a contemplative consciousness within us that enables us to be more present to all that is within and around us. It enables us to be more prayerful, more God-alert in our daily living. That is one way to become truly contemplative.

## Soul friends and other companions

Much has been written about the helpfulness of finding a spiritual guide or companion, what was called in the Celtic tradition a 'soul friend'. In the past this function was called spiritual direction. Many contemporary writers shy away from that title for a number of reasons. One is that it suggests the only part of a person's life that is important in such a relationship is the spiritual, whereas all aspects of our lives are, effectively, spiritual: the professional, the physical, the emotional, the artistic – all are part of what God created in us. The other is a distaste for the word 'direction'. This seems too much like having someone tell you what to do or putting your life into someone else's hands.

The great spiritual guides of the Christian tradition have had a very strong sense of being led themselves. In that respect, the relationship of spiritual direction is not a dual relationship but a triangular one, a ménage à trois, as it were. The real and only Spiritual Director is the Holy Spirit. Both the pilgrim/retreatant and the guide or companion are under the guidance of the same Spirit and both need to be obedient to that same Spirit. The Latin root of the word obedience is *ob-audire*, which means to listen attentively. The Chinese character for obedience contains parts of several other words: eyes, ears, heart, undivided attention and king. Obedience to the Holy Spirit requires us to be attentive to all aspects of our lives. It is not narcissism to ask myself how I am feeling, to wonder what gave rise to a particular reaction, to search for the root of a particular desire or to explore the dynamics of a given situation or relationship. All of this is data that will help me to become more aware of the ways in which I am either being drawn to greater faith, hope and love or being dragged away from them.

A wise guide can be a very helpful reality check as well as a voice of much-needed reassurance or challenge. It is not difficult to find people trained as spiritual companions, either by contacting a place of training or by searching on the internet. Some people, especially in a time of pandemic, have found it helpful to make retreats at home with a guide whom they can meet online. A list of where to look is available at the back of this book. No spiritual guides worth their salt think of themselves as legitimately having power over others in terms of being a guru or a spiritual expert. Should you ever meet someone who gives that impression, I would firmly recommend that you end the relationship at once.

Different authors have offered alternative analogies for the role of spiritual companion: midwife, gardener, accompanist are a few of them. The midwife's job is not to have the baby for the birthing mother but to provide reassurance and the knowledge that comes from experience, holding on when she is in pain or distress, telling her when to push or when to stop trying so hard, but primarily being there to help her to give birth to the new life that she is carrying. A good gardener does not spend all her time pulling up the plants by the roots to see how they are doing. She knows that there are times to water plants and times to leave them dry, letting nature take its own course; there are times for pruning and times to allow plants to grow or die at their own pace. The growth is the plant's, not the gardener's, though the gardener grows in wisdom and experience with each plant that she helps to flourish. A good accompanist knows that he is not the soloist. His job, by playing music in the background, is to keep the time and rhythm flowing so that the soloist can play or dance according to his own skill. An overpowering accompanist who gives way to the demands of his own ego ruins the solo performance. All of this gives some idea of the role of a spiritual guide.

In the story of the risen Jesus' appearance on the road to Emmaus in Luke's Gospel, Jesus meets two disciples discussing the story of the traumatic events of the past few days. The unrecognized Jesus doesn't attempt to give the disciples a moral or theological lesson, still less to tell them exactly what everything means. He simply gets them to tell him the story, then reflects on Scripture with them, allowing the Scriptures to interpret their lived reality, and their lived reality to shed light on the Scriptures. It's what is called in the theological business a 'hermeneutical circle'. It is at that point, when the disciples are able to put what they have experienced and what they have believed but not fully understood together, that they are able to recognize who it is who has been walking alongside them.

In his Spiritual Exercises, St Ignatius instructs the spiritual companion not to give lengthy theological explanations of any point to the person being accompanied: 'For it is not much knowledge that fills and satisfies the soul, but the intimate understanding and relish of the truth.'[4]

If you are taking time to make a retreat at home of whatever length, a spiritual companion, whether this be a book, an online community or an individual person, can be a valuable touchstone, able to help you with a reality check and offer kindness and reassurance or positive challenge when they are needed.

## The pilgrim and the guide

Having a spiritual companion at a time of retreat can be very helpful, for the reasons described, whether this is viewed as a long-term companionship or simply someone to walk along with us on this leg of the pilgrimage. Increasing numbers of well-trained companions can be found in real life but they can also be found in books and in the various sources of the Christian spiritual tradition, beginning with the desert solitaries whose words of wisdom and spiritual guidance were recorded and passed down in collections of sayings that would in later times become the foundation of the monastic life.

Spiritual reading comes in many forms, whether it's a matter of at last getting round to taking on one of the great spiritual classics, like the *Confessions* of St Augustine, John Bunyan's *Pilgrim's Progress* or the *Revelations of Divine Love* of Julian of Norwich, or engaging with something more contemporary. Many such books sit on people's bookshelves for years but they can seem like hard work on first acquaintance and so they are scarcely started and rarely finished. Perseverance with these texts, even if it is the consequence of making a contract with yourself to read a small extract slowly each day and to spend time reflecting on whatever you have understood of it, can become a real source of moving forwards in the spiritual life. Books written by twentieth-century spiritual authors like Etty Hillesum, Dietrich Bonhoeffer or Thomas Merton can have the same effect. Sometimes a commentator will take a classic text and edit and annotate it in such a way as to make it more easily accessible. Spending a period of time intentionally learning from an acknowledged spiritual teacher in this way is a different means of entering into spiritual companionship.

It may not be reading material from such sources but praying alongside others that feels like your best resource for spiritual companionship. The pandemic and subsequent lockdown has increased the use of communications technology, making it possible to share in the prayer of monastic houses and other intentional communities online. You may find ways of doing this that greatly support and strengthen your life of prayer. One word of warning is to remember that the liturgy is not a form of spectacle or entertainment. We have become so used to engaging with programmes on the television or other media provision on our computer screens that we can unwittingly end up engaging with such prayer and liturgy at a similarly low level of consciousness, while simultaneously knitting, writing out lists or running our eye over the daily newspaper. The excellent online resources for prayer currently available are not supplied as a form of pious entertainment but as a means to connect us with the things of God and with those who pray and seek alongside us. It's worth remembering that, even among hermits, the spiritual life is not for Lone Rangers. In Christian terms, God always calls us to community and is found within the community. While, essentially, a retreat is a personal process, travelling in companionship, whether with a present soul friend, someone from within the long tradition of Christian spirituality or someone online, will always make the journey lighter.

## Suggestions

- Look up one or other of the resources suggested for making the Examen. As well as those online (at: <www.ignatianspirituality.com/ignatian-prayer/the-examen>) you may wish to look at books like *Sleeping with Bread:*

*Holding what gives you life* by Dennis Linn, Sheila Fabricant Linn and Matthew Linn, or *A Simple, Life-Changing Prayer: Discovering the power of St. Ignatius Loyola's Examen* by Jim Manney.[5] They are available online both as paperback books and as electronic texts. As well as the Examen focusing on your inner life, there are some excellent versions of the Examen out there that have to do with issues of justice, peace and integrity of creation.[6]

- Consider beginning a personal journal, a prayer diary or a special photograph album or scrapbook as a meditative exercise. You may have a hidden artist within you who has never been allowed properly to surface. An excellent book to help your hidden artist emerge is *The Artist's Way: A spiritual path to higher creativity*, by American author Julia Cameron.[7] This kind of exercise is part of a spiritual and personal contract that you can make with yourself and with God to live more creatively and to pay more attention to your inner life and the life of God within you.

- Is there a spiritual book or author you have always been wanting to read but have never got round to engaging with? Perhaps now is the time to try. Some texts take perseverance, and it's generally best to start small and move on from there.

# 5

# Becoming a slow reader

The monastic Rule of St Benedict begins with the command to listen: 'Listen carefully, my child, to your master's precepts, and incline the ear of your heart.'[1] In fact, it is a quotation from the book of Proverbs (Proverbs 4.20). From the very beginning, the monk or nun is given to understand that listening is something that needs to be done with more than just the ears. Benedictine prayer revolves around the Scriptures, both in terms of the regular singing of the Divine Office, also called the *Opus Dei*, or work of God, and in terms of *lectio divina*, literally 'divine reading'. *Lectio* traces its origins back to early desert monasticism and has in recent years enjoyed a considerable resurgence of interest beyond the limits of monastic life. It isn't an intellectual practice or one engaged in principally for the purpose of theological exploration into a given text. When the practice originally arose, many of those who took it up on a daily basis had no books at their disposal and a number could not read at all. While the title suggests that this is a form of prayer that is undertaken by reading a text it could just as well be called divine listening as divine reading. It is less a question of reading the text and more a question of allowing oneself to be read by the text, as I suggested, in an earlier chapter, that we allow paintings or music or even the natural world to interrogate and teach us.

*Lectio* is an excellent way to spend a time of retreat. A short passage is read, sometimes aloud to a group and sometimes aloud or silently to oneself. Time is taken to allow the passage to percolate, with the flavour and significance of the passage trickling through slowly. The passage is read again and perhaps once more until it engages the heart fully and the reader can stay with whatever has emerged, perhaps just one word or one thread of an idea that weaves its way to a greater meaning.

Teachers of *lectio* point to a dynamic trajectory moving from the first hearing to the last. Traditionally, the stages of *lectio* (which travels more in a circular direction than a linear one) are:

- *lectio* (reading)
- *meditatio* (meditation)
- *oratio* (prayer)
- *contemplatio* (contemplation).

Reading seeks the direct meaning of the text, to allow its first impact through the story or teaching that it conveys. Meditation asks what this specific text is saying to me in my own context and circumstances, perhaps evoking significant memories or other texts, songs, conversations or ideas rising up to the surface of my mind. I may engage at the level of feeling or allow myself to see the text from different perspectives as it invites me to explore it from different angles. I may enter into the story myself and allow it to question me, relating it to some aspect of my own experience.

The purpose of all meditation on Scripture is that it should lead to an intimate encounter with God. How that encounter takes place and where it leads is God's business. Ours is to listen and to be open so that, in time, we can respond. The reading may evoke strong or even awkward-feeling reactions in us. This is not the moment to put on our polite manners for God, who deals in truth and reality, nor to assume behaviour reserved for dealing with a visiting dignitary or a revered elderly relative. God is not interested in the tidying up of our inner home to cover up the murky bits, but is far more likely, when coming into our space, to kick off his shoes, settle into the sagging old armchair and put his feet on the table.

Rather than adopting a polite veneer, it is important here to be as real and honest as possible. God is not troubled by the strength of our feelings, whatever type they may be. The Bible is full of people asking awkward questions, arguing with God, haggling and haranguing, reproaching and remonstrating. God takes it all without a blink. The letter to the Hebrews tells us that 'the word of God is living and active, sharper than any two-edged sword, piercing until it divides soul from spirit, joints from marrow; it is able to judge the thoughts and intentions of the heart' (Hebrews 4.12).

What is important is that we allow our responses and reactions to arise spontaneously, without any attempt to tidy them up or make them less unruly. A true friend is someone with whom we can share even our less than worthy thoughts and reactions. A true friend is also someone from whom we can hear difficult truths without being devastated by them or going off in an extended sulk or losing all sense of our own worth. Challenging truths offered in loving honesty can be the opening up of a whole new way of being ourselves. Above all, *lectio* is an exercise in truth, for it is only the truth that will set us free. The words of Scripture are an active principle, working in us like yeast in a loaf of bread. The words of the letter to the Hebrews suggest an effect that is quite forensic. The word doesn't allow itself to be manipulated or moulded to fit our own purposes. It lays bare, questions and challenges our heart's intentions in a way that can reveal for the first time what has lain hidden.

Contemplation follows on from our meditation on the word when we allow the Spirit, who inspires and speaks through the Scriptures, to be active in transforming our hearts and lives in line with the passage. This requires a willingness on our part to be transformed, to grow, let go or respond in a way that goes beyond words and touches the very fabric of our lives. Reading the Scriptures in this way isn't like reading a novel as a form of entertainment or a way of passing the time. It's a hazardous occupation, as is setting off on any journey of discovery. J. R. R. Tolkien's hero, the hobbit Bilbo Baggins, is a home-loving creature, deeply attached to his comfortable and predictable life. Horribly disconcerted to find himself at the centre of an unexpected adventure, he faces the unfamiliar and discovers hidden within himself unimagined resources of courage and resilience. He later warns his nephew Frodo that going out of one's door is a dangerous business, as the road may sweep one off anywhere.[2]

Prayer is always a risky business, but so is any form of growth beyond our limitations. It requires us to be willing to emerge from our comfort zone, ready to be changed by what we encounter. Like any other form of prayer, *lectio* will not leave us the same as we were when we began. If it does, it's unlikely to be the voice of God that we're hearing. Listening means paying active attention to whatever invitation, challenge, warning or wisdom the Scriptures offer us at a particular moment. Many of us are very good at not listening to what makes us feel uncomfortable. We make loud noises to cover up the 'still, small voice' that whispers insistently deep in our hearts, glossing over words or images that invite us to see things in a new way. We may find ourselves reading a passage that has become so familiar we barely notice what it says, then, suddenly, a hidden meaning is broken open and revealed. God has an impeccable sense of timing and sometimes it is simply that we are ready now in a way we were not before, to take on board what a given passage is saying to us and to act on what we hear.

## Zacchaeus: God has remembered

A brief example of the kind of process outlined above might be the story of Jesus meeting Zacchaeus in Luke's Gospel (19.1–8). Zacchaeus has made some serious compromises in his life that have not made him popular with his fellow Jews and have taken him far away from the faith in which he was brought up. He feels drawn to know Jesus better, but is prevented from doing so by his small stature, so he climbs a tree in order to look down. This also offers him a place to hide from the judgement of his peers and, possibly, of Jesus as well. Zacchaeus is hedging his bets, choosing whether or not to allow himself to be challenged by what he sees and hears. But Jesus is a greater risk-taker than Zacchaeus, risking becoming unpopular with a crowd (which includes his own disciples) that doesn't approve of his choice of company. He also risks being rejected by Zacchaeus himself, who may not want an uninvited dinner guest.

Reading this passage also challenges me. Like Zacchaeus, I may have compromised my values in order to be safe or to prosper. Perhaps my prosperity has meant others' loss. Who loses out to my gain? Zacchaeus is a figure of some authority. What model of authority have I used in my personal or working relationships? What has been the impact on other people of my being the person I am? The tree offers Zacchaeus a disguise, a place where the little man can hide. Is there a little person in me, desperate to hide? What makes me feel small? What do I normally do to make myself feel bigger? What would give me the courage to ask for healing so that I can be my real self? The tree also helps Zacchaeus to get perspective on Jesus. Have there been people or circumstances that have helped me to see Jesus more clearly and to get closer to him? How have I allowed that clarity to flourish? The name Zacchaeus means 'the Lord has remembered'. Jesus shows Zacchaeus that God has remembered who he really wants to be and recognizes the hidden good that his neighbours cannot see. He invites himself into Zacchaeus's home. What would it mean for me to invite Jesus into my space, my home? What does it mean for me to be invited to be where he is? If that meant moving out of my comfortable space, would I be willing to go?

Finally, Zacchaeus offers generous restitution to all those he has wronged. What kind of generosity do I habitually show when I realize that I have been in the wrong? We never hear the follow-up to Zacchaeus's encounter with Jesus, but we can be sure that he was never the same person again. From a relatively brief passage a great many responses arise when I allow myself to pay deep attention to the varied ways in which the story interrogates me.

When we allow the word of God to be turned loose on us, anything can happen. That is what makes prayer such an adventure. In his 'Exhortation on Sacred Scripture', *Verbum Domini,* Pope Benedict XVI outlines the stages of *lectio* as:

- **reading** what the biblical text says in itself, so that we avoid the risk of never moving beyond our own ideas;
- **meditating** on the text, so that we allow ourselves to be moved and challenged;
- **praying** in response to the word in such a way as to allow ourselves to be transformed;
- **contemplating**, in terms of seeing and judging reality with God's eyes and asking what conversion of mind, heart and life is being asked of us.[3]

## The renewal of our minds

Pope Benedict quotes the letter to the Romans, in which Paul tells us, 'Do not be conformed to this world, but be transformed by the renewing of your minds, so that you may discern what is the will of God – what is good and acceptable and perfect' (Romans 12.2).

What might it mean for me to have my mind renewed? It's easy for us to go along with the prevailing wisdom of the day without questioning what lies at the heart of contemporary culture. Many otherwise good, wise and holy people have gone along with levels of racial, gender or social prejudice that would appear totally unacceptable to those of a different generation, never questioning it because it is part of the social fabric in which they were brought up.

The German film *Downfall* is based on the memoirs of Hitler's former private secretary Traudl Junge, who went to work with him when she was a very young and inexperienced girl. The film portrays the gathering madness of Hitler during the final days in his bunker in Berlin in 1945, culminating in his death by suicide. It closes with an interview with the real Junge, now an old woman. She exonerates herself from any culpable involvement with Nazi ideology, citing her youth and inexperience as reasons why she didn't recognize in time the monster lurking within the admired Führer. However, she also reflects that Sophie Scholl, an anti-Nazi political activist within the White Rose student resistance group, was the same age as she was and took a different stance, ultimately giving her life for her opposition to all that Hitler stood for. Traudl Junge comes to admit that being young was not a sufficient excuse for not seeing what Nazism stemmed from and led to.

Being transformed by the renewal of our mind is a gift that we receive when we allow ourselves to be enlightened by Scripture, but it is not a passive process. We have to choose to be led by the Spirit of God, who speaks through Scripture, and to respond to the reality that it allows us to see. Ultimately, Pope Benedict says of the whole process of *lectio*, 'Contemplation aims at creating within us a truly wise and discerning vision of reality, as God sees it, and at forming within us "the mind of Christ" (1 Cor. 2:16). The word of God appears here as a criterion for discernment.[4]

Sophie Scholl and her companions saw with the eyes of faith the evil that lurked within Nazism and chose to act on what they saw, despite the mortal danger this involved. Pope Benedict adds a final, fifth stage of *actio* to *lectio*, a putting into action of whatever has resulted from this encounter with God through an attentive reading of the Scriptures: 'We do well also to remember that the process of *lectio divina* is not concluded until it arrives at action (*actio*), which moves the believer to make his or her life a gift for others in charity.'[5]

We may not be asked to die as martyrs, but close engagement with the word of God may demand that we enlarge our perspective and perhaps act in ways that are contrary to our natural pattern of behaviour or prior experience, giving up cherished patterns of thought and behaviour or taking on unexpected risks and sacrifices. This is unlikely to be about the grand heroic gesture. All over the world those who care for children, for sick and elderly relatives and spouses, key workers of every sort, give of themselves on a daily basis without counting the cost in order to make life possible for others. It is the everyday heroism of love made meaningful by service. When Jesus first met Peter and told him to cast his nets out one more time (Luke 5.4), the fisherman might have been justifiably irritated, wondering what this carpenter thought he knew about fish. But the catch resulting from his willingness to try was far more plentiful than Peter could ever have imagined. This is often how God rewards the risk that we take when we allow his word to get a grip on our lives. In the Gospels, Jesus is presented as the embodiment of the words that he speaks. He not only speaks the word, he *is* the Word. The Word not only has a voice but also a human face.[6] In the same way, we may find ourselves praying in such a way that we become the word that is spoken to us. It is part of our nature as human beings to have the capacity and the freedom to respond to God's word as it invites and challenges. As God's communication, it is always a dialogue in which

> we come to understand ourselves and we discover an answer to our heart's deepest questions. The word of God in fact is not inimical to us; it does not stifle our authentic desires, but rather illuminates them, purifies them and brings them to fulfilment.[7]

The more we familiarize ourselves in this way with the word of God, the more the word reveals us to ourselves and the more it gives us a language in which we can articulate what is deepest within us: 'The word of God draws each of us into a conversation with the Lord: the God who speaks teaches us how to speak to him.'[8]

God's word is never alien to us in its deepest sense, nor does it crush us, trying to make us someone different. It helps our authentic self to emerge, even if it does so by showing us the pretences and falsities that exist within our lives. This way of internalizing the word of God becomes transformative of us at depth. It changes the ways that we relate to God, to ourselves, to others and to our world. It is the best way to ensure that the word becomes flesh.

## Suggestions

- Take time to look at the stages of *lectio divina* described in this chapter. There are numerous websites and even YouTube sessions on it, but it is better for you to allow yourself to try it: *lectio* is not a spectator sport!

- Find a short biblical passage, perhaps Mark 10.46–52, Luke 8.43–48, Luke 1.26–38 or Isaiah 43.1–4. Take time to relax and become still, according to one or other of the earlier relaxation exercises in this book. Allow yourself at least 15 minutes to read the passage. Even if you become bored and can think of hundreds of more important things to do, you have offered this time to God and to yourself, so keep your end of the bargain. If 'nothing happens', you will at least know that you gave God some time. Remember that the word of God doing its work may not be evident immediately.

- When you have finished your time of attentiveness and prayer, come slowly out of it and take time to review the prayer, noting anything that strikes you. Notice where your imagination led and, especially, what feeling responses emerged.

# 6

# A picture is worth a thousand words

*Lectio divina* is a time-honoured way to pray with the word of God that connects us with over a thousand years of monastic tradition. Internalizing the word of God becomes transformative of us at depth, changing the way that we relate to God, to ourselves, to others and to our world. It is the best way to ensure that the word 'becomes flesh' in the reality of our lives. Our best pattern for this is found in Mary, the mother of Jesus. In its narrative about the birth of Jesus, Luke's Gospel tells us: 'As for Mary, she treasured all these things and pondered them in her heart' (Luke 2.19, NJB).

This doesn't mean that Mary had some direct personal revelation which made it easy and automatic for her to understand everything going on within and around her. No one can honestly imagine that the journey from Nazareth to Bethlehem while in the last stages of pregnancy can have been anything but grim. To arrive, finally, only to discover that she is going to have to give birth to her first child in the dirt and smell of a stable cannot in any way have been good news. It did not get much more reassuring as time went on. We don't know how historically accurate the infancy narratives in the Gospels are, but their tales of child massacre and sudden flight into refugee status are also not good news in any human sense. We have only to see the desperate images on our television screens of similar dramas being played out across the world to understand the human cost involved. The stories of the presentation of Jesus in the Temple in Jerusalem and then, 12 years later, the losing and finding of the boy Jesus make it clear that pondering the word of God was not simply a matter for Mary of thinking happy, re-assuring thoughts. She is told by Simeon that a sword will pierce her heart and when she is finally reunited with her lost son, her cry of bewilderment and hurt will sound famil-iar to any parent confronted with incomprehensible adoles-cent behaviour: 'My child, why have you done this to us? See how worried your father and I have been' (Luke 2.48, njb).

Yet, later on, we also see how this pondering of the word attuned Mary to her son's mission, even when, humanly speaking, she had no idea how he would choose to act on it. At the wedding feast of Cana, she is sensitive to the human needs within a difficult social situation and instinctively turns to her son. Despite his seeming reluctance, and his apparent refusal to respond to her plea, she knows very well who it is she's dealing with and trusts that his very presence will bring about transformation in some way. 'Do whatever he tells you' (John 2.5) are the words of someone who is on God's wavelength, who has learned to trust in God's trans-formative power, even when it at first appears as if nothing is going to change at all. This is the level of trust to which we are invited when we find ourselves called into encounter with the word of God.

Another way to ponder God's word is through the use of our imagination. Imaginative contemplation is more commonly associated with the Spiritual Exercises of Ignatius of Loyola, though, like the monks of old, he himself elaborated on an earlier tradition. Ignatius's own conversion began during a long convalescence from a battle injury when he began reading a *Life of Christ* and the *Lives of the Saints* for want of more exciting reading material.[1] He recognized a notable difference between his response to texts like these and the tales of chivalry that were his preferred form of reading. He noticed that when he immersed himself in a tale of knightly derring-do, with swashbuckling heroes and beautiful damsels in distress, the initial impact of the story was strong and he was able to respond fully to the excitement and passion of the tale, but afterwards that passion faded and he was left feeling jaded and empty. His spiritual reading had an almost diametrically opposite effect. It was much harder going to begin with, as it was a much less stimulating read with regard to his desires and passions, but it left him imagining how he might respond to the insistent call within the narratives that continued to have a transformative effect long after he had closed the book.

Ignatius found himself imagining that he might be a second St Francis or St Dominic. What might he find himself doing for God if he were? He began longing to love, serve and transform the world in response to the call to arms of Christ the eternal King rather than to that of an earthly ruler. His reading led him to articulate and understand his own deepest desires, beyond the heroic fantasies based on his own ego, and to find the strength to act on them. Having recovered, he began a pilgrim journey that took him to a cave in Manresa, where he lived in a rigorous, self-imposed solitary retreat which nearly drove him mad. This is emphatically not what is being advocated here in this book. He was eventually saved by the wise companionship of an elderly lay woman living in the area and by the re-emergence of his own good sense. Through the use of his imagination, Ignatius began to find a way of engaging heart and soul with the biblical stories of encounter with Jesus himself, entering into the scene and allowing the story to take him over. Allowing the story itself to be the agent, and following wherever the story happened to lead, noticing every word and emotion in response, he learned the transformative power of word and mental image in drawing him close to God and revealing his inner thoughts to himself.

In his Spiritual Exercises, Ignatius teaches us to articulate our own longings through assimilation of those that are expressed in the encounters with Jesus in the Bible. 'What do you want me to do for you?' asks Jesus of those who approach him. 'Lord, if you will, you can make me clean, you can raise what is dead, you can restore my sight, you can satisfy my hunger, you can heal me and drive out what is dark within me.' Jesus acts, though not always in the way that we expect. He speaks, and his words are both comfort and challenge. They may take us by surprise, as may our own reactions to him. People who have been unquestioningly religious, conforming to religious ideas and practice without ever really investigating them, can find themselves angry and outraged by something that Jesus says or does. His actions and words may appear questionable, as they did to many of those who witnessed them. 'How can this man speak like this?' they ask. 'Why have you done this?' Even those who loved and revered Jesus asked such questions. Our own hidden resentments or unhealed hurts may rise to the surface, as may our doubts and anxieties and uncertainties about this God who takes us by surprise. In this respect it is the text that interrogates us rather than the other way round, and that can be a very healthy thing, if also a disconcerting one. Exploring our reactions with a skilled companion can also allow us to articulate to ourselves what lies beneath our responses. We can see this dynamic unfolding in the following conversation between Michael, a man who has been learning to pray with imaginative contemplation, and his spiritual companion, Helen.

## A spiritual conversation

HELEN: So Michael, you found yourself witnessing Jesus telling the story of the prodigal son. What happened?

MICHAEL: I didn't enter into the story itself, becoming one of the brothers or anything like that. Instead, I found myself on the edge of the crowd, watching what was going on, and listening to the story Jesus was telling.

HELEN: You were just an onlooker?

MICHAEL: Yes. At first it was OK, I just went along with the story as Jesus told it, but I found myself getting more and more irritated by it or, at least, frustrated by the father's attitude.

HELEN: The way the father was acting upset you in some way?

MICHAEL: Mmm. I think it's because it reminded me of the situation at home. I'm the eldest in our family and my dad was disabled quite early on in life, so I had to take on a lot of responsibility for my mum and siblings. I wanted to go to art school, but instead I had to take a job in a haulage firm, which I hated, but it brought in the money. I was very much the dutiful son and, in most ways, I did it willingly – I love my family and was proud to be able to help them. People were always saying, 'I don't know what they would do without you', and I liked that, but somewhere deep down I would be thinking, 'But what about me? What about my hopes and dreams?'

HELEN: You felt as if the real you wasn't getting a look-in?

MICHAEL: Yes, I felt as if I had sort of disappeared. In the end my own needs just got swallowed up by those of the family. It didn't help that my younger brother went off the rails. He got into drugs and all sorts of trouble. I was very angry with him for the upset he caused my parents and it made me feel as if my sacrifice was being wasted.

HELEN: And the Gospel story brought this all up to the surface?

MICHAEL: Yes, and I found myself wanting to shout at the father and at the younger brother. The older brother in the story seems to get a raw deal. He's the one who's dutiful and conscientious. He does what the father wants and he takes his share of the responsibilities, but it's the younger brother who turns out to be the 'hero' when he's done nothing but waste the family money and cause a lot of grief.

HELEN: Like your brother? And you felt angry about that?

MICHAEL: I found myself resenting how unfair it all was. I wanted the father to take care of the son for a change, rather than the other way round.

HELEN: Were you able to say that to Jesus?

MICHAEL: At first I didn't dare. I mean, this is God we're talking about, right? But then I remembered how you said to respond in any way that I wanted and not to let myself be held back, so I really let go and told him what I thought of his story – I had a real go at him.

HELEN: And how did that feel?

MICHAEL: It felt really liberating, actually. I felt I was able to be real with him in a way that I'd never been able to be real with my own father, because of his disability. I was always shielding him, so that in some way I became the parent and he became the child. Jesus' words in the story came back to me in a very different way. I felt as if the father was thanking me, trusting me, and now he was encouraging me to embrace life in the way that I really wanted and had never been able to do before. It was as if I was being given permission.

HELEN: Permission to . . .

MICHAEL: Permission to be the me I've always wanted to be. Permission to liberate my inner artist (*laughs*) and not always to be the good boy.

HELEN: You're proposing to go off the rails yourself?

MICHAEL: (*laughs*) No, I haven't got the energy for that, but I realize how narrow my life has become and how much resentment has built up in me. I have a sense of Jesus inviting me to let go of that and to explore different possibilities. I think that could be good. I'd like to give it a try, anyway.

Through the exercise of imaginative contemplation of Scripture, Michael has learned to admit and accept his need for inner liberation. This is another word for growth in humanity and holiness. In his apostolic exhortation *Gaudete et Exsultate* ('Rejoice and be Glad'), Pope Francis writes:

> Do not be afraid to set your sights higher, to allow yourself to be loved and liberated by God. Do not be afraid to let yourself be guided by the Holy Spirit. Holiness does not make you less human, since it is an encounter between your weakness and the power of God's grace.[2]

Most people don't think of aspiring to holiness. It seems too weird, too out of the ordinary and too 'out of this world' to feel normal or comfortable. But if we understand it as being set free from what prevents us from being most deeply ourselves, an invitation to become truly human beings, then we can see holiness as something eminently normal, profoundly real and a reasonable thing to desire and hope for. Imaginative contemplation can lead us to a way of being real with God and ourselves that shifts our horizons from conventional religiosity to something alive, vibrant and transformative. It can be a helpful daily practice, but some focused time to do this in a retreat situation, whether alone at home or in a supported context, can help us to develop this spiritual capacity as a habit.

## Feedback

Contemporary life is full of feedback forms – they can often be a tiresome burden, a pointless exercise made up by the public relations sector in a given firm or institution, required only in order for the institution to congratulate itself on achieving its own targets. But this is not about assessing our own spiritual performance. At the end of any time of prayer it's good to do a review as a bridge between prayer time and ordinary time so that we can remember, while it's still fresh in our memory, what struck us particularly or what response seems to be inviting us in a specific direction. It's disruptive to just leap up as soon as we've come out of a time of prayer and go hurtling into the next task. Instead, we should take a bit of 'decompression' time and allow ourselves to reflect on what has been happening. Taking time to make a cup of something and then mulling things over while drinking it can help, but so can doing the laundry or digging the garden or tidying a drawer – anything that doesn't require very sustained thought so as to give room for our own post-prayer thoughts to breathe. The most important thing is to mark the transition from prayer to review in some way and to change your mode of communication, so if you have been sitting in conversation with God, move to writing or drawing, for example. It's also worth inviting God to the party and asking for the gift of memory and insight to see whatever God wants you to notice and recognize as significant.

You might ask yourself some of the following questions.

- Have I had any sense of a pattern emerging, something linking up with previous times of prayer or reflection, with questions or trains of thought that have been at the back (or forefront) of my mind of late, with an emerging desire or sense of invitation or avoidance?

- Do I have any words or images to describe the prayer? Does it remind me of a song or a poem, or a feeling that I can trace back to some other source beginning to gain more solid outlines? Where are my feelings right now? Where were they during the prayer?
- Has there been any sense of resistance or disturbance, invitation or attraction that needs to be looked into? Was I able to 'stay put' or did my mind wander off into various distractions? Did I have a sense of God's or my absence or presence?
- Did I have any strong negative reactions? Can I name those for what they were, and what provoked them? Was I able to acknowledge them and talk freely to God about them? Where do they seem to be leading?
- If I had a conversation with God, what was it about? Did I find myself asking for any particular grace or gift? Was there any sense of growing in faith, hope or love, or of shrinking back into myself?
- Do I have a sense of anything coming to life (or of something trying to hide or needing to die)? How does that make me feel?
- Is any action required that follows on from this time of prayer? Is there anything that might prevent me from taking this kind of action?

Finally, I give thanks for any insight I have received, reflect on it and make some kind of note of it, so that later on I can see where this insight led or how I got diverted from it.

## Suggestions

- Give yourself an opportunity to try imaginative contemplation. There are many websites and books, from various religious perspectives, that offer guidance with this. You will find an excellent short video by James Martin SJ at: <www.ignatianspirituality.com/ignatian-contemplation>.
- There is also a very helpful short article by David L. Fleming SJ, entitled 'Pray with Your Imagination', available at: <www.ignatianspirituality.com/ignatian-prayer/the-spiritual-exercises/pray-with-your-imagination>. Even if you think you have no imagination, it's worth giving it a try. At the end of the time you have set, take the opportunity to have a conversation with God and ask for whatever gift or grace you seem particularly to need.
- You will also find other kinds of imaginative contemplation, not based on biblical stories, in the work of Anthony de Mello, an Indian Jesuit priest and psychotherapist. His book, *Sadhana: A way to God – Christian exercises in Eastern form*,[3] encourages visualization and the use of imaginative contemplation, introducing resources from East and West. It may be unfamiliar territory for some, but is well worth exploring as a means of seeing how the use of imagination in prayer can be a helpful way to meet God personally.

# 7

# Choose life

From the moment we wake up to the moment when we fall asleep, we are making choices, some of them trivial and incidental, others involving the building up or deconstructing of good or bad habits that may have a significant impact on the rest of our lives. How we choose to live our daily lives, even in the small details, can play a major role in how we either grow into the fullest version of who God created us to be or dwindle and diminish into a shell of that person. Few people get out of bed in the morning and idly decide to get married, start up a company, commit a murder or cheat on their spouse or partner. Both positive and negative decisions are usually the cumulative build-up over time of smaller choices that might appear insignificant in themselves. Choices for inner freedom take time, which is why the Twelve Steps programme speaks of taking recovery one day at a time. The choice not to drink or fall into addictive behaviour may only be for this morning but may last through till the afternoon and on into the next day and the next, building up into a lifetime of recovery and sobriety. The choice to enter into recovery may be made at one point in our personal history but it needs to go on being made progressively if it is to hold good.

We make our major life decisions in linear time, on a particular date – to get married, enter into a profession or move abroad – but we also go on constantly reiterating and refining or reshaping these decisions as we grow and change. We make decisions and then spend time growing into them. Many of us make life promises without any real notion of what the living out of those promises might entail. Only time and experience teach us what we have taken on. Life itself is never simply the repetition of the same cycle one year after another. We live in a permanent state of becoming, so that the more we live, the more we become the person we are in the process of turning into.

In the book of Deuteronomy, Moses presents the people with a stark choice: will they choose to live in relationship with God (life and prosperity) or will they go their own way (death and adversity)? He warns them that their choice will have consequences and urges them to choose life (Deuteronomy 30.15–20). We rarely get confronted with such clear alternatives, and as the centuries rolled on, the choice to live in covenant with God became more complex against the background of political, economic and religious movements of the day. Being God's people did not bring with it an unmistakable blueprint for personal or national behaviour and they were left having to use their wits, relying on their instincts like everyone else. Believing in God does not give us a safe package deal on how to live a trouble-free existence, but faith gives us the assurance that the Holy Spirit is at work within us and, by nature, we have the capacity to make choices which are in tune with the mind of God.

In his letter to the Philippians Paul says, 'Let the same mind be in you that was in Christ Jesus.' This is a significant challenge. How do we know what was in the mind of Jesus at any given point? The inner workings of his mind, even when we read the Gospels, are generally hidden from us, much as the inner workings of our own minds can be a mystery even to ourselves. Paul offers Jesus' habitual patterns of choice as guidance for his followers as he goes on to speak of Jesus emptying himself and becoming obedient to the point of death (Philippians 2.5–8). We considered earlier in this book that obedience is another way of saying 'being attentive'. Attentive to the Father's will, Jesus emptied himself of power from the moment of his incarnation to the moment of his death on the cross. He continues to empty himself of power by allowing us the freedom to make our own choices, great and small. This is both a gift and the most enormous challenge.

The Spiritual Exercises of St Ignatius are based on the desire to become free from disordered attachments. It is natural that we become grateful for the gifts, skills and aptitudes we recognize God has given us, nurturing such capacities in ourselves in a way that makes us more fully human. This only becomes a problem when we cannot function without the feel-good factor that comes from being recognized, praised and looked up to because of them. If we begin to need the compensation of food, drink, pornography, excitement, power or someone else's constant affirmation to help us continue to play whatever role we define ourselves by, we have what Ignatius calls a 'disordered attachment'. It can turn into addictive or dependent behaviour that, ultimately, becomes destructive of ourselves and those around us. The various ways to pray and spend focused retreat time advocated in this book can help to redress a balance that may be in danger of getting lost.

## Readjusting the focus

One word for getting things into better focus is discernment. Discernment is not a magical formula for getting every choice and decision right but is a way to practise making choices in small things so that listening for the voice of the Spirit becomes a habit of awareness and reflectiveness which will serve us well when it comes to the bigger choices as well as the general orientation of our lives.

The COVID-19 pandemic that began in 2020 pulled many people's lives apart in ways that were experienced as shattering and destructive of human society as we know it. But while, on the one hand, this will have had lasting and devastating consequences, on the other it has also provided some opportunities for rebalancing lives that had become oppressive in subtle ways. The Chinese character for crisis is made up of the signs for danger and for opportunity: both are aspects of the same situation, depending on how we respond. Part of the purpose of any retreat is to discover a deeper truth about our lives and how we are responding to all the graces, challenges and opportunities that are part of God's providence. We seek to refocus and rebalance, exploring the healthiness or otherwise of our own personal lives, or maybe seek to adjust our distance vision, reading the signs of the times in order to work out how we are being invited to live in response to those signs. St Paul writes about the guidance of the Spirit, contrasting the fearful 'spirit of slavery' with the 'spirit of adoption' that enables us to recognize the presence of God, our loving Father. He describes creation itself as 'subjected to futility . . . [in a] bondage to decay'. In other words, things don't always work as they should, falling into disarray and failing, despite our best efforts. But all is not lost:

> the Spirit helps us in our weakness; for we do not know how to pray as we ought, but that very Spirit intercedes with sighs too deep for words. And God, who searches the heart, knows what is the mind of the Spirit, because the Spirit intercedes for the saints according to the will of God. We know that all things work together for good for those who love God, who are called according to his purpose.
> (Romans 8.14–28)

This is not some easy and well-meaning optimism. Paul himself lived a life full of challenge, danger and disappointing frustrations. A difficult character to work alongside, those who were supposed to help him often misunderstood or failed him and he found himself in repeated opposition to the very people he most hoped to convince. What he says about the Spirit here bears consideration for its significance for our own lives in the present day. We see, from the everyday panorama of conflicts and social or natural disasters filling our television screens, that life can often be precarious. Faith does not operate as a safety blanket but as the source of a deep strength enabling us to make good choices about how to weather life's storms. Paul appeals to that sense of rootedness in the God to whom we belong, as children to a loving parent, so that, come what may, we know God will never let us go and God will give us the graces and inner resources we need to survive and flourish.

# Finding the 'spirit level'

Paul is a realist who knows how difficult life can be, even (or perhaps especially) for those who have entrusted their lives to God. Elsewhere he comments: 'We are afflicted in every way, but not crushed; perplexed, but not driven to despair; persecuted, but not forsaken; struck down, but not destroyed' (2 Corinthians 4.8–9). These are the words of someone who has come to reflect on every aspect of his life from the perspective of the Holy Spirit. St Ignatius also speaks about the Spirit or, rather, about good and evil spirits. Such language may sound alien to the modern mind, but there is a profound wisdom in the way he sees human beings operating. Like most of his contemporaries, Ignatius believed that the world and human affairs were ruled by good and bad spirits. Our era tends to use a different vocabulary to describe the same aspects of the human condition. In his 'Rules for the Discernment of Spirits' for the first 'Week' of his Spiritual Exercises,[1] Ignatius refers to 'the enemy', meaning different aspects of personal evil within the universe that operate both within and beyond our selves. His analysis of how this phenomenon manifests itself is down to earth and pragmatic and shows a sound understanding of human psychology.

Ignatius sees someone in the grip of disordered attachment of any kind as an ego that is out of control, ruled by what he calls sensual delights and gratifications. This person will be strongly attracted to apparent pleasures, so that the strategy of the enemy is to make what is ultimately toxic look increasingly attractive. In speaking of the Spirit of God, Ignatius refers to the 'good spirit'. For a person in the grip of the evil spirit, the operation of the good spirit will tend to be experienced as something initially negative. A disturbing sense of dis-ease, a stinging conscience, a sense of futility, regret and remorse are all, in this context, a sign of the good spirit at work, though not necessarily pleasant in themselves. Ironically, what makes us feel uncomfortable and uneasy in this context may prove the incentive we need to take better control of our lives and admit that we have a problem which needs to be faced and dealt with.

Conversely, when a person is normally living a good life under the guidance of the Holy Spirit, then it is characteristic of the enemy to afflict such a person with anxiety, depression and a sense of helplessness grounded in what Ignatius calls 'fallacious reasonings that disturb the soul'.[2] Some forms of depression may be an indication that a person is unwell and in need of professional help, but this is the sort of loss of hope, self-confidence and courage that can afflict people even when there is no evidence of psychological illness of any kind. When Ignatius speaks in this context in terms of consolation and desolation, he is not talking about feeling happy or feeling sad. A person going from bad to worse may feel perfectly happy living a life of total selfishness and destructive indulgence. Asking 'How do you feel?' may not elicit any sense of self-awareness or of moral balance. Becoming aware of the workings of the Holy Spirit may, for such a person, be a distinctly disturbing and un-comfortable experience, even though, ultimately, it leads to liberation and human flourishing. Understood this way, on the one hand disturbance may be the best thing that can happen to the person. On the other hand, for a person lead-ing a God-centred life, the action of the Holy Spirit is likely to be gentle and reassuring, even in the midst of challenging and difficult circumstances. Such a person is 'at home' with God, so the entrance of the Holy Spirit is like that of some-one walking into the room in a way that feels familiar and unobtrusive. Whatever causes disturbance and struggle in such a person is unlikely to be of God.

A person's image of God may have become distorted in a way that turns God into a disappointed parent, a bully or a punishing tyrant. This may lead to the person suffering from what has been termed 'hardening of the oughteries'. Such a person may be far more in need of a happy day sit-ting on a beach eating ice-cream than of pushing herself even further in pursuit of what she perceives to be good. A time of retreat and reflectiveness may help a person to realize that he has adopted ways of thinking, speaking or behaving that, ultimately, are destructive and self-defeating. He may realize that he needs to step off the treadmill and give himself space to live and think in a way that is more life-giving for himself and for those around him.

## Discernment: a toolkit

The development of a capacity for discernment generally requires a regular habit of serious prayer and reflection that would include paying attention to affective responses in relation to encounters with God in Scripture or in any other form of prayer and spiritual engagement. Making well-discerned choices also requires the ordinary human elements of adequate information, weighing reasons for and against a particular option and confirmation over time that a decision taken sits well with reality. A discerning person needs to be equipped with self-knowledge, self-acceptance, the ability to integrate dreams and desires with the reality of the lived context, and the validation that comes from sharing these thought processes with wise and trusted friends and companions.

In the biblical narratives, we see people like Moses, David, Mary and Joseph, Peter, Paul, and Martha trying to make sense of their experiences, moving forwards without certainty and often at great cost to themselves. It can help to read their stories, even though we don't get a full picture, seeing them grow from fear to freedom. We can discern the trajectory of our own stories by asking ourselves questions that we would want to ask them.

*Question. Can you remember any time in your own story when you have come to a choice or decision after struggling for clarity? What was the process by which you came to this choice? What made it easy and what made it difficult?*

In discerning the right decision, some key points may help to clarify where and by what inner paths we are being led. First, our desires matter. An image of God that tells us we are not allowed to have desires of our own will not be helpful, any more than will our using God to legitimize whatever our plans may be. Finding out what we truly want and being willing to engage with those desires can be a challenge, especially if we are not used to connecting with our desires. Equally, we may find ourselves being invited to let go of certain dreams and desires if they have become rigid and compulsive. If we find ourselves thinking or saying to God, 'I will only ever be happy if . . .', then we are cutting off whole possibilities by insisting that we are the only source of wisdom here. In the garden of Gethsemane, we see Jesus afraid, not wanting to die. He admits this to himself and his Father, but places himself trustfully into the Father's hands. Paradoxically, this handing over of his own will leads to the freedom and authority that he displays through his entire trial and crucifixion. This is far more easily said than done, but it is possible for us to learn to let go of our 'devices and desires' in pursuit of the greater freedom of being in tune with God's will at work in ourselves.

**Question**. *What makes it easy for you to get in touch with your desires? What makes it difficult? If you have found yourself acting on a deep desire, what gave you the incentive to do so?*

If our desires matter, then our questions also matter, whether they be practical/information questions, without which we cannot make a well-grounded choice, or our own inner questions, denoting a level of uncertainty or misgiving. A key part of discernment is to know what lies at the heart of our questions. Are there fears and anxieties there, an inability to let go and walk forwards in trust? The fact that we are uncertain does not always carry negative implications. It may be that, in our heart of hearts, we don't want to make a choice that has been wished on us by others or by circumstances. If we have not been used to having our own desires taken seriously, we may need to find courage to admit to ourselves that we have preferences. If we have always been used to being the decision-maker, we may need to become more sensitive to the unspoken hopes, fears or objections in others.

*Question. Have you ever found yourself questioning an established narrative about yourself? 'I'm hopeless at . . .' 'You'll never make it in . . .' 'No one in our family has ever . . .' What has made it possible for you to overcome such narratives and find inner confidence? Have you ever found yourself asking questions that reveal hidden misgivings or hesitations about something that otherwise seems good? What wisdom have you learned from allowing yourself to ask such questions?*

If our desires and questions are not neutral, nor are our memories. We can find that we are captive to certain memories or the memory of patterns in our lives that have not served us well. By the same token, the memory of our deepest encounters with God can also help us to reconnect with what lies at the root of our heart's desire and our most authentic self.

*Question. Can you think of a context in which memory has served you well or ill when trying to come to a choice or decision?*

Having adequate information and reliable self-knowledge is a crucial part of making trustworthy decisions. But sometimes one has to make a leap of faith, based not on rational thought so much as on intuition. In this sense, we need to learn to take our instincts and intuitions seriously. If we have had a 'sort of feeling' over a long period or recognize a pattern of orientation towards a particular choice that will not let go of us, it is worth exploring this as the guiding light of God's Spirit. It may also be worth taking our dreams seriously in this context as they reveal from our unconscious mind hidden desires or fears that can be essential data in our decision-making. We may also need to pay attention to unadmitted negative feelings. What kind of information might they offer us?

Reason and imagination are not opposites: they are different faculties of the mind that enable us to get in touch with responses to God's grace which are both affective and the fruit of careful consideration.

*Question. Have you ever made a choice or decision based on instinct or intuition rather than on rational thinking? How did you learn to trust that intuition? In what ways do you see (a) reason and (b) imagination working in the context of discernment?*

If our desires and questions, memories and intuitions must be taken seriously in a process of discernment then so also should our body. Our physical bodies are powerful carriers of wisdom. All sense experience is data for discernment and most of it comes to us first through our bodies, which can be a source of God's revelation. Even our language tells us something important about the wisdom carried by our bodies. When we talk about being unable to swallow something, feeling choked, about something being a pain or giving us a headache, we may be speaking figuratively but also revealing a point of tension within the physical self that reveals unresolved conflicts and anxieties to which the conscious mind is not yet attuned. All of this needs to be taken into account if we are to make reliable choices.

*Question. Can you think of a time when you have experienced your body as a 'carrier of wisdom' in this context? What did you learn from taking your body seriously? If you find yourself frequently ignoring physical signs of this sort, why is that?*

Sometimes, however hard we try to discern according to the promptings of the Holy Spirit, time and experience prove that we were mistaken in our judgement in a given instance. It may simply be that circumstances are beyond our control and we cannot make 'the right choice'; we can only make the least bad choice. Sometimes we gain greater wisdom from our failures and mistakes than from our successes. This, in its own way, is a form of discernment when we learn to put our trust in God, whatever the outcome. Confirmation of a choice made can be found in the Scriptures and in the doctrine and moral teaching of the Church. It can also be found in the wisdom and experience of the faith community or that of family, colleagues and friends. It takes courage and inner freedom to face the answer, but we can ask ourselves what the most frequent criticism is when we receive it. Can we see any truth in that criticism? Is someone holding up a mirror to us of the way we habitually speak or behave that is open to question? We don't have to take everyone's criticism as Revealed Truth, but it would be foolish never to listen to the critical comments of friends and colleagues. It may help us occasionally to play devil's advocate and to place that criticism in opposition to a choice that we are making. Does this choice conform to a pattern that others perceive as negative? Am I just going for the same old option repeatedly? Or am I jumping at innovation for its own sake, without valuing what I already have?

**Question**. *What do you understand by confirmation in this context? Have you ever received confirmation of a choice or decision that helped you to go forward with it? Or have you ever made a choice and then gone back on it because time in reflection showed it not to have been wise? What made it easy or difficult for you to accept the confirmation that you received?*

There are factors that can prove to be an obstacle to good discernment. Poor physical or emotional health might suggest that we need sufficient rest and relaxation or recovery time to enable us to pray and reflect seriously. The aftermath of a major loss or bereavement, or the breakdown of a significant relationship, is not a good context for making choices and decisions requiring inner freedom. It is important that we take our emotions seriously before engaging in discernment. We may have formed attachments or compulsions that prevent us from being able to exercise freedom of mind and will. This is also important when it comes to having rigid attitudes, whether they be patterns of religious thinking or prejudices to which we cling – none of this makes for freedom of spirit.

We may have become disconnected from feelings and memories that make us feel uncomfortable, or we may have got out of practice in using our imagination. This will make the charting of our affective responses difficult, as will being dominated by fears and anxieties or social and cultural factors that make it hard for us to think broadly. The development of a discerning heart is something that happens over a long period of time. Prayer helps with this, as does the regular practice of the Examen of consciousness, spiritual journalling, the healing of memories, and spiritual conversation with a trusted companion. All of these can be part of a retreat or retreat practices engaged in over time, which help us to grow in spiritual wisdom. Some people enter into retreat with the express purpose of coming to a momentous decision. Sometimes it turns out that they are not so much coming to a decision as coming to accept and acknowledge a decision already made, though that news has not yet reached their brain. It is often best in retreat not to focus on the decision itself, but to 'park' it in a corner, where it can be acknowledged and treated with respect but not made the sole focus of attention. We can then get on with the business of familiarizing ourselves with Jesus and becoming his companion in whatever way of prayer suits us best. When the time is right, the choice often emerges organically, without having had to become the focus of a specific or separate process. It's as if the decision creeps up on us and makes its presence felt without us having noticed that we are making it.

## Suggestions

- Explore one or more of the questions posed in this chapter. You may like to do so just by thinking reflectively or by journalling or having a spiritual conversation with a trusted companion. What emerges from your exploration?

- In terms of prayer, you may find it helpful to spend time in the company of someone like Peter, a very vivid character in the New Testament who offers us a concrete picture of someone growing slowly in discernment. With Peter's impulsive character it's often a question of two steps forwards, one step back, but we can see a marked pattern of spiritual growth over the narratives. You may find it helpful to sketch out in writing the trajectory of Peter's responses and reactions, mapping out why you think he speaks or reacts as he does, what seems to change his mind, how his choice affects the rest of his life as a follower of Jesus. Try looking at the Bible passages below as a series of sketches of Peter's development as a disciple. What patterns of growth in faith and understanding do you see in him? In what ways might some of these patterns stand as an archetype for us as disciples?

| Luke 5.1–10 | Matthew 14.23–31 | Matthew 16.13–25 | Luke 9.28–35 |
|---|---|---|---|
| John 6.60–69 | Luke 18.22–34 | Luke 22.31–34 | Matthew 26.37–45 |
| Luke 22.54–62 | John 20.1–8 | John 21.15–19 | Acts 3.2–8 |
| Acts 5.12–15 | Acts 10.9–15 | Galatians 2.9–14 | |

- You may also find this book helpful: J. Michael Sparough SJ, Tim Hipskind SJ and Jim Manney, *What's Your Decision? How to make choices with confidence and clarity*.[3] There is helpful material on group discernment in an article by William J. Byron at: <www.ignatian spirituality.com/making-good-decisions/an-approach-to-good-choices/a-method-of-group-decision-making>.

# Conclusion

## It's not all about me

Towards the end of his Spiritual Exercises, St Ignatius states: 'Love ought to find its expression in deeds rather than in words.'[1] He says this in the context of a set-piece contemplation that prompts those making a retreat to reflect on all the gifts they have received from God and to find within themselves a corresponding desire to offer service in return. Much of this book has been about how to make space on an occasional or regular basis to develop retreat practices, whether in the short or long term. We have talked about becoming more reflective, exploring our inner life and personal relationship with God and asking God to free us from whatever prevents us from living life to the full. These are all excellent goals, but the Christian understanding of discipleship does not allow them to become a form of spiritual narcissism. There is more to all this than a programme of self-improvement, however effective. We need to go beyond such a goal and ask ourselves what we are being improved for. The simple answer is: service of God and of the world God created.

Any serious engagement in prayer – whether it involves using music, art and the bodily senses or poetry and other forms of literature, the natural world or the Scriptures themselves – not only shifts our focus inwards but, if it is to be truly Christian, will also shift our focus back outwards.

The French motto of *reculer pour mieux sauter* may mean taking a step backwards in order to make a greater leap forwards, but it also implies going inwards the better subsequently to focus outwards. The Spanish mystic St John of the Cross might be seen as one of the world's foremost exponents of the type of contemplative prayer that has its roots in abandonment of the world with its pleasures and preoccupations. In fact, he said that the ultimate goal of mystical prayer is love. The English mystic Julian of Norwich comes to the conclusion at the end of her *Revelations of Divine Love* that love was Jesus' principal purpose in appearing to her in her mystical visions. The true contemplative life never becomes self-preoccupied but involves liberation from egoism of every sort and has love as its ultimate goal. This includes the call to action on behalf of justice and peace, even if that action is prayer itself, undertaken in withdrawal and solitude for the good of the world.

The first 'Week' of the Ignatian Spiritual Exercises is aimed at helping retreatants to know and experience themselves as loved and forgiven sinners. This understanding is followed by a reflection on the call of Christ the King. The retreatant, who has focused principally on his or her own inner life and personal story, is called by Jesus to join him in the great enterprise of saving and transforming the world. This means entering personally into God's plan and desire for the world to be as its Creator intended. Later on, the retreatant is invited to pray the meditation on the Two Standards, which contrasts the methods of Jesus and Satan in attracting followers to achieve their aims. The test of authenticity of any spiritual insight or mystical experience will be how successfully it draws the one gifted with it to discipleship. How closely has this person assimilated the vision and saving purpose of Jesus in the incarnation? This does not necessarily mean that everyone making a retreat will inevitably drop everything at the end of it and go off to be a missionary in far-flung parts of the globe. It does not preclude a return to 'ordinary' life, except that the practice of retreat reveals to us that there is no such thing as ordinary life. All life lived in relationship with God is revealed as extraordinary, as laden with mystery and capable of miraculous transformation. This may be in the simple context of our daily relationships or of work that seems humdrum and banal to our own eyes. Yet it's possible to live sanctity as a waitress, a hospital porter or a shelf-stacker in a supermarket as much as it is in a monastery or a hermitage.

The practice of retreat sharpens our perceptions and tunes our senses not only to the presence of God but also to any human situation where godly perspectives and values have been abandoned in pursuit of profit and the advantage of the few at the cost of the many. Part of any retreat, and the Examen of consciousness that goes with it, needs to include a personal appraisal of the state of the world, and trying to find out what God may be inviting us to do about it. It may lead us to a more committed engagement with lobbying for social justice by writing to political leaders and representatives, joining online petitions or large-scale movements. But it could just as well mean going to help an elderly neighbour, contributing to the local food bank or adjusting our consumer habits in favour of more ethical buying. The invitation may be to eat and cook more ethically, to be more committed to ecological justice or to support anti-trafficking initiatives.

At one point in the Spiritual Exercises, the retreatant is encouraged to ask: 'What have I done for Christ? What am I doing for Christ? What will I do for Christ?'[2] This whole book and its encouragement to develop retreat practices at home implicitly asks the same questions. This is rooted in the belief that each of us is unique. There is a me-shaped hole in the universe that only I can fill. It makes a difference whether I am here or not. Retreat practices help us to discover more deeply who we are so that we can fulfil the purpose for which God created us. If there is a final conclusion to this book, it consists of a plea not to develop such practices for our own gratification. We may find ourselves living calmer and more balanced and purposeful lives as a result, and that is always good, but the wider world needs to feel the benefit of these practices too. It will do so if, by building retreat times into our lives, we become transformed transformers, sharing God's dream for the world and putting ourselves at God's service for turning that dream into a reality.

# Further reading

Barry, William A., *Praying the Truth: Deepening your friendship with God through honest prayer* (Chicago, IL: Loyola Press, 2012).

Cameron, Julia, *The Artist's Way: A spiritual path to higher creativity* (London: Souvenir Press, 2020).

Cameron, Julia, *The Listening Path: The creative art of attention – a six-week artist's way programme* (London: Souvenir Press, 2021).

Martin, James, *The Jesuit Guide to (Almost) Everything: A spirituality for real life* (New York: HarperCollins, 2012).

Muldoon, Tim, *The Ignatian Workout: Daily spiritual exercises for a healthy faith* (Chicago, IL: Loyola Press, 2004).

Simmonds, Gemma, *The Way of Ignatius* (London: SPCK, 2019).

Thibodeaux, Mark E., *Reimagining the Ignatian Examen* (Chicago, IL: Loyola Press, 2015).

# Notes

## Introduction

1 Pope Benedict XVI, *Spe Salvi* (2007), 2. (Available online at: <www.vatican.va/content/benedict-xvi/en/encyclicals/documents/hf_ben-xvi_enc_20071130_spe-salvi.html>.)

## 1 Fantastic retreats and how to find them

1 See <www.campaigntoendloneliness.org/the-facts-on-loneliness>.

2 See <www.alcoholics-anonymous.org.uk/About-AA/The-12-Steps-of-AA>.

3 Gerard W. Hughes, *God of Surprises* (London: Darton, Longman & Todd, 1985), p. x.

4 Köder's images can be found online, but see also <www.paulineuk.org/koder> for resources on Sieger Köder, including Gemma Simmonds, *The Closeness of God* (Slough: Pauline Books and Media), a book of meditative reflections that includes one on Jacob.

5 See <http://orientations.jesuits.ca/bob/page1.htm#review>.

## 2 Making room

1 Rob Parsons, *The Heart of Success: Making it in business without losing in life* (London: Hodder & Stoughton, 2009).

2 You can find a version of Ignatius's Principal and Foundation in paragraph 23 of his Spiritual Exercises at *The Spiritual Exercises*, trans. Louis J. Puhl SJ, <http://

spex.ignatianspirituality.com/SpiritualExercises/Puhl>. All subsequent references to the Spiritual Exercises will be from this version and referenced by paragraph under the title of *Sp.Exx.*

3 Jean-Pierre De Caussade, *The Sacrament of the Present Moment*, trans. Kitty Muggeridge (London: Collins, 1981).

4 'God's Grandeur' in *Gerard Manley Hopkins: Poems and prose* (London: Penguin, 1985).

5 For excellent help regarding how to go about this, see the Ignatian spirituality website, at: <www.ignatianspirituality.com>.

## 3 An 'inside the body' experience

1 'Keep young and beautiful', lyrics by Al Dubin.

2 See <www.poemhunter.com/poem/no-man-is-an-island>.

3 See <www.parkwestgallery.com/francisco-goya-disasters-of-war>.

4 See <www.fnal.gov>.

5 The same Preparatory Exercises and reflective review will be helpful with poetry and literature as with other sources of reflection.

6 See Paul Murray, *Aquinas at Prayer: The Bible, mysticism and poetry* (London: A & C Black, 2013).

## 4 The examined life

1 See <http://reimaginingexamen.ignatianspirituality.com> and Mark E. Thibodeaux, *Reimagining the Ignatian Examen* (Chicago, IL: Loyola Press, 2015).

2 Pope Francis, *Evangelii Gaudium* (2013), 49. (Available online at: <www.vatican.va/content/francesco/en/

apost_exhortations/documents/papa-francesco_
esortazione-ap_20131124_evangelii-gaudium.html>).

3 Matthew 6.34, *The Passion Translation*.

4 *Sp.Exx.* 2.

5 Dennis Linn, Sheila Fabricant Linn and Matthew Linn,
*Sleeping with Bread: Holding what gives you life* (Mahwah,
NJ: Paulist Press, 1995); Jim Manney, *A Simple, Life-
Changing Prayer: Discovering the power of St. Ignatius
Loyola's Examen* (Chicago, IL: Loyola Press, 2011).

6 See the 'Reimagining the Ignatian Examen' app (at: <http://
reimaginingexamen.ignatianspirituality.com>).

7 Julia Cameron, *The Artist's Way: A spiritual path to higher
creativity* (New York: Jeremy P. Tarcher, 1992).

## 5 Becoming a slow reader

1 Leonard J. Doyle (ed.), *Saint Benedict's Rule for Monasteries*
(Collegeville, MN: Liturgical Press, 1950).

2 See J. R. R. Tolkien, *The Lord of the Rings: The Fellowship
of the Ring: Book 1* (London: HarperCollins, 2011),
Chapter 3.

3 Pope Benedict XVI, *Verbum Domini* (2010), 87 (my
paraphrase). (Available online at: <www.vatican.va/
content/benedict-xvi/en/apost_exhortations/documents/
hf_ben-xvi_exh_20100930_verbum-domini.html>.)

4 Benedict XVI, *Verbum Domini*, 87.

5 Benedict XVI, *Verbum Domini*, 87.

6 Benedict XVI, *Verbum Domini*, 12

7 Benedict XVI, *Verbum Domini*, 23

8 Benedict XVI, *Verbum Domini*, 24

## 6 A picture is worth a thousand words

1 Ludolph of Saxony, *Vita Jesu Christi*; Jacobus de Voragine, *Flos Sanctorum*.
2 Pope Francis, *Gaudete et Exsultate* (2018), 34. (Available online at: <www.vatican.va/content/francesco/en/apost_exhortations/documents/papa-francesco_esortazione-ap_20180319_gaudete-et-exsultate.html>.)
3 Anthony de Mello, *Sadhana: A way to God – Christian exercises in Eastern form* (New York: Image, 1997).

## 7 Choose life

1 *Sp.Exx.* 314–15.
2 *Sp.Exx.* 315.
3 J. Michael Sparough SJ, Tim Hipskind SJ and Jim Manney, *What's Your Decision? How to make choices with confidence and clarity* (Chicago, IL: Loyola University Press, 2010).

## Conclusion

1 *Sp.Exx.* 230.
2 *Sp.Exx.* 53.

# FORM IS A SPIRITUAL
# FORMATION IMPRINT
# OF SPCK

As well as being an award-winning publisher, SPCK is the oldest Anglican mission agency in the world.

Our mission is to lead the way in creating books and resources that help everyone to make sense of faith.

Will you partner with us to put good books into the hands of prisoners, great assemblies in front of schoolchildren, help create small groups resources for our Home Groups website and reach out to people who have not yet been touched by the Christian faith?

**To donate, please visit www.spckpublishing.co.uk/donate or call our friendly fundraising team on 020 7592 3900.**